RADICAL & FREE

MUSINGS ON THE RELIGIOUS LIFE

BRIAN O'LEARY SJ

MESSENGER
PUBLICATIONS
JESUITS *in* IRELAND

First published 2016 by Messenger Publications

ISBN 978 1 910248 38 6

Designed by Messenger Publications Design Department
Typeset in Baskerville
Printed by W & G Baird Ltd

Messenger Publications,
37 Lower Leeson Street, Dublin 2
www.messenger.ie

Contents

Prologue

The Pope Francis Factor

Pope Francis proclaimed a Year of Consecrated Life in an Apostolic Letter dated 21 November 2014.[1] It was to begin on the First Sunday of Advent that year and conclude on the Feast of the Presentation of Jesus in the Temple, 2 February 2016. This particular time was chosen because it was the fiftieth anniversary of two key documents from Vatican II – that on the Church *(Lumen Gentium)* and that on the up-to-date renewal of religious life *(Perfectae Caritatis)*. Francis clearly wanted the Year of Consecrated Life to be an ecclesial event. He stressed this, saying, 'The Year of Consecrated Life concerns not only consecrated persons, but the entire Church'. All the People of God were called to celebrate the existence among them of those men and women living one or other of the various forms of consecrated life.

Of the many initiatives undertaken by Pope Francis this was one of the least spectacular, perhaps even one of the least effective. It did not grab people's imagination or spark their enthusiasm to any great extent. Compared with the current Year of Mercy it was low-key, if not almost 'under the radar'. Reasons for this outcome are not difficult to find. In the western world (the main context for these reflections) consecrated life is in a condition of serious diminishment. Its image (and reality) is currently one of ageing men and women, increasingly fragile, overburdened with responsibilities, coping heroically in an increasingly secular culture that no longer understands the rationale of their lives. They have become isolated and peripheral to a society in which they had formerly been fully integrated and hugely esteemed.

The miracle (I use the word deliberately) is that so many of these women and men remain people of deep faith and undiluted hope. In the midst of their struggles they have taken to heart the Lord's words to the apostle Paul: 'My grace is sufficient for you, for power is made perfect in weakness'. (2 Cor 12:9) Their witness is indispensable for their fellow Christians today because the Church too is suffering diminishment in its personnel, status and influence. The consecrated life has thus become a benchmark or point of reference for the experience of the People of God as a whole. Far from becoming irrelevant, the consecrated life is assuming a new and unexpected role in the Church simply by accepting and enduring its present-day passion with serenity – even with joy.

We are well accustomed to recognising the centrality of joy in the teaching of Pope Francis, ever since his 2013 Apostolic Exhortation *Evangelii Gaudium* (the joy of the gospel). Consequently it is not surprising that he speaks again of joy in his Apostolic Letter proclaiming the Year of Consecrated Life.

> That old saying will always be true, 'Where there are religious, there is joy.' We are called to know and show that God is able to fill our hearts to the brim with happiness; that we need not seek our happiness elsewhere; that the authentic fraternity found in our communities increases our joy; and that our total self-giving in service to the church, to families and young people, to the elderly and the poor, brings us life-long personal fulfilment. None of us should be dour, discontented and dissatisfied, for 'a gloomy disciple is a disciple of gloom'. (II.1)

But Francis is no sentimental dreamer. He is well aware of the difficult circumstances in which the consecrated life has to be lived today. Like everyone else, we have our troubles, our dark nights of the soul, our disappointments and infirmities, our experience of slowing down as we grow older. But in all these things we should be able to discover 'perfect joy'. For it is here that we learn to recognise the face of Christ, who became like us in all things, and to rejoice in the knowledge that we are being conformed to him who, out of love of us, did not refuse the sufferings of the cross.

Genesis of this Book

As ways to mark the Year of Consecrated Life I was invited to offer two preached retreats in 2015. The first, of eight days, took place at Loreto Centre in Llandudno, while the second, over four days, was hosted by Manresa House, the Jesuit Centre of Spirituality in Dublin. The talks that I gave on these two occasions form the basis for this book. In preparing them I incorporated material harvested in teaching a course on consecrated life over a period of 30 years at the Milltown Institute. However, I did not regard my retreat presentations at Loreto and Manresa as lectures in an academic sense. Retreat talks are aimed at leading listeners into personal reflection and prayer. They are meant to be evocative and suggestive rather than didactic and systematic. On the other hand, I did not want to offer purely devotional material without any intellectual substance behind it. Our minds, as well as our hearts, play their part in our spiritual lives. The result is a series of considerations or 'musings' (see the book's sub-title) that aimed at being prayerful but that drew on the wisdom of the Bible, insights from the history of consecrated life, and suitable theological reflections.

In readying these talks for publication in book format, most of the changes I made relate to matters of style (such as eliminating expressions that were overly conversational). The substance of the talks has remained intact, although amended wherever that seemed necessary. I have also given references to works from which I quote, and added occasional footnotes of my own. But I have kept these to a minimum. However, there is one specific change in terminology which I need to explain briefly.

Consecrated Life and Religious Life

What Pope Francis promulgated in 2014 was a Year of Consecrated Life. This term, 'consecrated life', is relatively new. It was first used in an official Church document in the revised Code of Canon Law (1983) where Part III of Book II, *The People of God*, has the heading 'Institutes of Consecrated Life and Societies of Apostolic Life'. In this context 'consecrated life' embraces institutes of religious life, secular institutes, hermits or anchorites, and the order of virgins (but not societies of apostolic life). The 1994 Synod of Bishops reflected on the theme 'The Consecrated Life and its Role in the Church and in the World', which was followed by Pope St John Paul II's response and exhortation, *Vita Consecrata*. All this confirmed the contemporary meaning of the term. Nonetheless, John Paul also included societies of apostolic life in his reflections, showing that the categories found in the Code are not rigid. It is clear that Pope Francis was equally inclusive in his use of the term.

During the two retreats I used the term consecrated life throughout. I was deliberately trying to encourage celebration of the *many* manifestations of consecrated life, rather than narrowing the focus to religious life alone. however, in this book i have chosen to revert to the more common term. As the Year of Consecrated Life is over, I no longer feel obliged to keep reminding readers of the fuller diversity that exists in the Church. I am certainly not denying its reality or underestimating its richness. However, women and men committed to the religious life constitute by far the most numerous exponents of the consecrated life, making it also the most readily recognisable. This book is primarily about them, their motivations and their values. Furthermore, I discovered that linguistically the term religious life was easier to use, for the simple reason that 'religious' can serve as a noun (singular and plural) as well as an adjective. There is no corresponding noun to describe someone in the (wider) consecrated life. In my presentations I had found myself straining to find ways of referring to such a person, using roundabout phrases but with clumsy results.

Plan of the Book

After an opening chapter on the origins of religious life, the rest of the book is built around the three traditional vows (poverty, chastity, obedience). Each is given two chapters. This may seem to some an overly conventional or predictable way of presenting religious life today. However, I have discovered that probing the meaning of the vows not only uncovers the deeper significance (often hidden) of religious life, but constitutes a surprisingly comprehensive methodology. What concerns me throughout are values rather than structures. Values are perennial, rooted in Christian faith. While they certainly have to be incarnated in structures that are historically conditioned, the values underpinning the vows always provide the core of religious life. Finally, I have no confidence in futurology (attempting to see what religious life may look like in the future). Only God knows that secret, and it may be wise to wait in patient hope until it is revealed.

CHAPTER 1

The Origins of Religious Life

Ressourcement

One of the most far-reaching mandates of Vatican II was that Catholics return to the sources of their faith; that they engage in *ressourcement*. For all believers that meant fostering study of the Bible, the Patristic tradition and liturgical practice since New Testament times. For religious it also meant a reawakening and reclaiming of their particular charism as expressed in the lives of their founders and the early documents of their Institutes. Only when they had engaged adequately with this *ressourcement* could they move into an authentic *aggiornamento*, an updating and renewal of the structures, practices and even attitudes that they had inherited from more recent times. By and large religious men and women have done this task well, in spite of all the diminishments that they have experienced over the same time span. It is even tempting to say that some religious have brought about, not simply an *aggiornamento*, not even simply a renewal, but a genuine refounding of their institutes.

However, my intention is to reflect, not on the origins of individual orders or congregations, but on those of Christian religious life itself. It is often pointed out nowadays that something analogous to what we call religious life exists in all the major religions of the world. The very mention of Buddhism evokes colourful images of saffron-robed monks engaged in meditation or work in their monasteries. The Dalai Lama is widely admired across traditions as a wise spiritual leader. In Hinduism a life of total renunciation *(sanyasi)* can be traced back to the Upanishadic period and still flourishes today. Sufism is the mystical branch of Islam and Sufis are those who devote their lives to engaging directly with this tradition. Their best-known representative among westerners today is the thirteenth-century scholar and poet, Rumi.

Thomas Merton discovered for himself the value of dialogue between the Christian monastic tradition and those of the great Asian religions. Many others have followed Merton's lead. Meditation has been a particularly fruitful topic in such conversations. But to say that all these traditions are analogous, or even that their practitioners share an appreciation of the spiritual, or have a common sense of liminality,[1] is not to claim that they are all the same or that they are somehow interchangeable. Each is embedded in the specific beliefs and/or philosophy of its own religion, and none exists apart from that underlying foundation. In simple terms, Christian religious life is based on Christ, the Word made flesh, who died and is now risen and exalted. Hence it cannot be understood (still less lived) apart from him and the Spirit-filled Church that guarantees his continuing presence in our world.

Beginnings

There is no clear consensus as to when Christian religious life can be said to have begun. Some want to root it as far back as the New Testament period. They point to evidence that some Christians, mostly women, chose to live a life of virginity or, when widowed, a life of celibate chastity rather than remarry. These virgins and widows devoted their lives to prayer and to the service of the Christian community.

Some may have lived together for mutual support but most seem to have continued living with their families. This first-century phenomenon is without doubt an expression of a life consecrated to God, but to take it as the historical beginnings of religious life is problematic. Those who do so also tend to use this New Testament evidence to argue that celibate chastity is the core value in religious life. But is this universally true? Has it been the experience of all Christian religious? This question is certainly worth pondering. However, since it is so profoundly personal, it may be better not to seek a general answer but to invite all religious to answer for themselves. What is the core value in *my* religious life?

The more widely accepted understanding of the beginnings of religious life situates it in the movement of men and women ascetics into the Judean, Syrian and Egyptian deserts.[2] This was happening from as early as the second century but gained momentum from the late third century. The first ascetics tended to live as solitaries or anchorites. Among these the Abba Antony (251–356) was the best known and most influential.[3] However, the majority chose to live as cenobites, i.e. in community. Abba Pachomius (292–348), Antony's near contemporary, was the first great monastic legislator. Both styles of living (anchoritic and cenobitic) were the soil in which what became known as the Wisdom of the Desert grew and flourished. This tradition played an important role in the development of discernment of spirits, both its practice and the emerging theology underpinning it. Ignatius Loyola tapped into this ancient source as he composed the Spiritual Exercises, especially the Rules for Discernment.[4]

The Symbolism of Desert

The interpretive key (both for discernment of spirits and for these early forms of religious life) lies in the double symbolism of the desert in the Bible. On the one hand, the desert is the place where a people, or

11

an individual, meets God, especially in a time of crisis. Crossing the desert during the Exodus, as they escaped from slavery in Egypt, the Hebrews knew that they had found favour with God. This is sometimes called the honeymoon period of their mutual relationship both because of their heightened awareness of God's closeness to them and the delight that they took in this intimacy. On the other hand, the desert has a darker, more sinister symbolic meaning. It is the natural habitat of the evil spirits, hence a location where spiritual combat becomes inevitable. Those who go into the desert are deliberately taking on the demons on their own home territory, where the fighting can be expected to be face-to-face and ferocious.

It is difficult to determine the precise motivations of those who chose to live in the desert. Most likely, as in the personal stories of all religious, their motivations were mixed. Many different influences were in play during that period of history. For some Christians the desert served initially as a haven from persecution. But once they began to grow accustomed to the harsh environment, some of them decided to stay on with the aim of cultivating a life of holiness. A different situation arose after the end of the persecutions. Constantine's Edict of Milan (313) granted toleration for Christians throughout the Empire. Now the desert offered something quite different – an alternative to life in the cities, which were seen as infected by a climate of moral depravity, or at least of mediocrity. In the desert, on the other hand, a fully authentic Christian life could be lived unhindered. Furthermore, in some cases, especially in Egypt, economic factors played a part. Poor Egyptian peasants found in the desert an escape from the insurmountable economic burdens they carried on their farms and in their villages.

Martyrdom

Finally, we come to the most intriguing and potentially controversial motivation of all: the ascetic life of the desert as an alternative to martyrdom. During the first three centuries of the Church's history, the era of the persecutions, the most representative (even archetypal) Christian spirituality was that of martyrdom. The martyr who witnessed to Christ by willingly accepting a violent death, became (in the imagery and rhetoric of the age) the perfect imitator of Christ himself, the true disciple, the mighty athlete of God, the great champion of the Christian host in its conflict with the devil. The most powerful expression of this spirituality comes from the letters of Ignatius, Bishop of Antioch (c.35–107). He was condemned to death during the reign of the Emperor Trajan (53–117) and sent in chains to Rome to be slaughtered by wild animals in the Flavian amphitheatre. On this journey Ignatius wrote ahead to the Church in Rome begging the Christians there not to try to secure his release.

> For my part, I am writing to all the churches and assuring them that I am truly in earnest about dying for God – if only you yourselves put no obstacles in the way. I must implore you to do me no such untimely kindness; pray leave me to be a meal for the beasts, for it is they who can provide my way to God. I am his wheat, ground fine by the lions' teeth to be made purest bread for Christ … When there is no trace of my body left for the world to see, then I shall truly be Jesus Christ's disciple. So intercede with Him for me, that by their instrumentality I may be made a sacrifice to God. (4)[5]

Further on in the letter he adds:

> All the ends of the earth, all the kingdoms of the world would be of no profit to me; so far as I am concerned, to die in Jesus Christ is better than to be monarch of earth's widest bounds. He who died for us is all that I seek; he who rose again for us is my whole desire. The pangs of birth are upon me; have patience with me, my

brothers and sisters, and do not shut me out from life, do not wish me to be stillborn ... Leave me to imitate the Passion of my God. (6)[6]

Here we see the conviction, not unique to Ignatius of Antioch, that the day of a martyr's death is their *dies natalis*, the day of their birth into the fullness of life. The pattern of Christ's death, embodied in the martyr, is transformed into the pattern of Christ's resurrection.

Some today find this spirituality to be morbid, fanatical and repugnant. They may even suspect it of bordering on the heretical, with its apparent disdain for the value and beauty of (one's own) human life. The current distortion and manipulation of the notion of martyrdom in extremist Islam (turning it into a weapon for mass murder) only adds to this uneasiness. However, we might ask if anyone who has not experienced the Christian martyrs' overwhelming desire to be with Christ is in a position to judge? In spite of the disturbing imagery he conjures up, Ignatius is reaching out and longing, not primarily for death, but for Christ. Death is merely the gateway through which he has to pass. Rowan Williams is a strong defender of Ignatius and his spirituality.

It is not difficult to accuse Ignatius of morbidity and pathological exaggeration in his attitude towards his coming death; but what makes such an accusation appear shallow and entirely inadequate is the absence in these letters of anything that might be described as self-hatred, and the profound sense in their author that his martyrdom is the climax of his *gift* to the Church of himself. It is here that Ignatius is most deeply united with Paul and with the New Testament in general – in the conviction that fleshly life is not a burden to be borne, nor a prison to be escaped from, but a task to be perfected in grace. It is, indeed (borrowing Eliot's phrase), 'a symbol perfected in death', but only in a death made significant by its relation to the whole of a *life*. So that the life which is marked by service, compassion, poverty, acceptance and so forth is no less intrinsically significant than the death in which it ends, is in fact not separable from it.[7]

Spiritual Martyrdom

A spirituality of martyrdom is only realistic in a literal sense so long as physical martyrdom is a real possibility. But the persecution of Christians in the early Church gradually became more sporadic until it eventually ceased entirely. It was during this transitional period that a new theology of 'spiritual' or 'white' martyrdom began to emerge. This aimed at nurturing a desire for union with Christ that was just as strong as that of the martyrs. However, it was to be expressed, not through the enduring of a violent, physical death, but through other kinds of suffering patiently borne in imitation of the martyrs, and ultimately in imitation of Christ. These sufferings could range from illness and disability to the hatred and hostility of one's enemies or of the evil spirits. Above all, they could be identified with the struggles and the dying-to-self associated with the ascetic life – whether lived by anchorites or cenobites.

Some writers have questioned the degree to which this spirituality of martyrdom inspired the Desert Fathers and Mothers. It is surely correct to say that it did not provide their sole motivation (I have already suggested that their motives were mixed). Nevertheless, it is hard to deny that it was, to a significant degree, influential among them. For instance, in the literature of the desert there is a fascinating series of parallels drawn between martyrs and monks.

    ☛ Martyrs were described as *athletes* of Christ. The same term was also applied to monks. Here the tradition was taking up a Pauline theme in which a comparison is drawn between the strivings necessary in the Christian life on the one hand, and in athletic training and competition on the other. (1 Cor 9:24–27)

☛ Similarly, martyrs and monks were equally considered to be *soldiers* of Christ. They were both engaged in a *militia spiritualis*, a spiritual military service. Here, too, there is an obvious Pauline background – his theme of the spiritual combat. (Eph 6:10–13) The synoptic gospels present Jesus himself as battling with Satan in the desert. (Lk 4:1–13)

☛ From these biblically based terminologies we turn to a powerful symbol or prophetic gesture. A monk would sometimes be buried, at his own request, in the same grave as a martyr. Lying side by side in death, the monk and the martyr gave common testimony to their love of Christ and their faith in the resurrection.

☛ Later in the tradition, as martyrdom came to be regarded as a second baptism, monastic profession came to be understood in the same way. Like the martyr at his death, the monk at his profession was said to die to the world, and to rise with Christ to a new and holy life.

☛ Finally, there is the theme of the bride of Christ. Building on the Old Testament portrayal of Israel as the bride of God, (Jer 3:8; Hos 2:16; Is 54:4–10), the New Testament described the Church as the bride of Christ. (Eph 5:25–27; 2 Cor 11:2; Rev 19:7–9, 21:10) Early Christian writers, working with this same metaphor, described virgin-martyrs such as St Agnes, St Barbara and St Lucy as brides of Christ (as much because of their martyrdom as because of their virginity). But eventually, beginning in the patristic period, this imagery was applied, not only to virgin-martyrs, but to all consecrated virgins.

Antony the Great

A key source for understanding the spirituality of the desert is *The Life of Antony* by Saint Athanasius.[8] The author and his subject were in fact friends, although their personalities and life experience could hardly have been more dissimilar. Antony was a hermit or solitary, seeking God directly through spiritual experience and ascetic discipline. Athanasius was not only bishop of a major see in the Mediterranean world but a learned and sophisticated theologian. Antony belonged to the oral tradition of the desert, exemplified by the relationship between an abba or amma and their disciples. Athanasius was a product of the literary tradition from which came the writings of the great Church Fathers. But in spite of these differences the two men shared a mutual respect and warmth. However, Athanasius' admiration was not only for his friend Antony, but for the whole way of life that he represented. So, in composing his *Life of Antony*, he was not attempting a biography in our modern sense, but an *apologia* for the way of life that was emerging in the desert – an *apologia* for religious life in its origins. His description of Antony's original call is memorable in itself, but it also presents a paradigm for the way in which religious have heard and responded to their call over the centuries.

> He was left alone, after his parents' death, with one quite young sister. He was about eighteen or even twenty years old, and he was responsible both for the home and his sister. Six months had not passed since the death of his parents when, going to the Lord's house as usual and gathering his thoughts, he considered while he walked how the apostles, forsaking everything, followed

the Saviour, and how in Acts some sold what they pos-
sessed and took the proceeds and placed them at the feet
of the apostles for distribution among those in need, and
what great hope is stored up for such people in heaven.
He went into the church pondering these things, and
just then it happened that the gospel was being read,
and he heard the Lord saying to the rich man, 'If you
would be perfect, go, sell what you possess and give to
the poor, and you will have treasure in heaven'. It was as
if by God's design he held the saints in his recollection,
and as if the passage were read on his account. (2)

In this vividly portrayed scenario there is no reference to martyrdom but to three gospel stories that sparked the young Antony into a
radical conversion (not from a bad life to a good one, but from a good
life to a better one).

☛ Firstly, Antony's attention is drawn to the call of the
apostles. (as in Mt 4:18–22)

☛ Then he is challenged by the summary passages in
the early chapters of the Acts of the Apostles which
speak of renunciation of one's possessions in favour of
the poor. (Acts 2:42–47; 4:32–37)

☛ Finally, he hears the story of the Rich Young Man,
which impinged on him as though it had been addressed
personally to himself. (Mt 19:16–22)

In every period of the Church's history these New Testament passages – the call of the apostles, the life of the early Christian community in Jerusalem, and the story of the Rich Young Man – are
constantly referred to whenever religious speak of their experience
of vocation. They somehow encapsulate the focus, the energy and
the continuity of the tradition. They are like a golden thread running
through it, even as the outer forms of religious life were continually

evolving and being reconfigured. Athanasius had astutely seen to the heart of the matter, to the values that were to last.

Conclusion

This exercise in *ressourcement*, this journey to revisit the origins of religious life, has brought us into contact with a culture and mentality profoundly different from our own. We need a certain historical imagination, along with a generosity of spirit, to enter into this world and appreciate what it is offering us. But the rewards are immense. Perhaps what is most astonishing about these early desert ascetics is that they did not see themselves as doing anything extraordinary. They may have had a number of motivations for moving to the desert, but behind them all was a humble desire and a resolute determination to model their lives on that of Jesus and to embrace the gospel in its fullness. They were not adding anything to it but simply seeking an environment in which they could live it with the greatest freedom and integrity.

CHAPTER 2

The Biblical Roots of Poverty

Triad of Evangelical Counsels

The emergence of poverty, chastity and obedience as a triad to represent the substance of religious life was a relatively late development. In the Desert tradition the all-embracing term 'to renounce' had sufficed. Monks were those who had 'made their renunciation', which implicitly included renunciation of their ownership of material goods, of marriage, and of self-will. To this (especially in cenobitic communities) was shortly added the phrase, 'living according to the Rule'. With the later spread of Latin, monks were known as 'regulars', those living under a *regula* or Rule. However, the emergence of distinct evangelical counsels, along with their corresponding vows, did not begin until the Middle Ages.

Two texts are particularly important as evidence for this medieval development. The first is a personal letter written in 1148 by Odo, abbot of St Geneviève in Paris, an abbey that followed the Rule of St Augustine. Although the vocabulary was still evolving, Odo's letter shed light on what later became the classic terminology. He wrote: 'In our profession we promise three things, as you well know, chastity, sharing, obedience.' The Latin word translated here as 'sharing' is *communio*. We get a clearer understanding of what this word meant for Odo towards the beginning of the Rule of St Augustine: 'You should live in the house in unity of spirit and you should have one soul and one heart centred on God. And then, you should not call anything your own, but you should have everything in common' (I.2,3).[1] In short, unity or *communio*, the ideal of sharing their lives together, requires, but is not exhausted by, the common ownership and use of material goods.

The second text is a letter from Pope Innocent III (1198–1216) to the abbot of the Benedictine monastery at Subiaco. Innocent immersed himself in every aspect of the life of the Church, including the spiritual well-being of monks. In 1202, half a century after Odo's letter, Innocent made a canonical visit to Subiaco, and on his return to Rome wrote this letter to the abbot. He expressed concern about several deficiencies he had witnessed, and set down criteria for authentic monastic living. The critical passage for us reads:

> The renunciation of property *(abdicatio proprietatis)*, as also the custody of chastity *(custodia castitatis)*, is so connected to the monastic rule *(regulae monachali)*, that not even the Supreme Pontiff can dispense in its regard.

The reference to the monastic rule can be taken as another way of speaking of obedience. The terminology is still fluid. Two consequences of this papal letter are noteworthy. Firstly, its teaching becomes normative for all subsequent Benedictine reform. Secondly, and of wider consequence, it declares that these three named values are indispensable to the religious life.

In both letters, that of Odo and that of Innocent, the word 'poverty' is not yet in use. Instead we find two different terms: sharing *(communio)* and renunciation of property. If we add the phrase from the Rule of St Augustine about not calling anything one's own, we have a third. These are not exactly interchangeable terms but each underlines a particular aspect of the value or virtue in question. This multi-faceted nature of poverty is something I will return to in the next chapter. Indeed, over the centuries the various facets of poverty have continued to multiply. But the main point here is that, for both Odo and Innocent, poverty (however it is described) forms part of a triad. These we now call the evangelical counsels. Later in the thirteenth century Thomas Aquinas will freely use the word 'poverty'. In his *Summa Theologiae* he taught that the foundation of charity is 'voluntary poverty *(voluntaria paupertas)* so that one may live without anything of one's own *(absque proprio)'* (2a 2ae q. 186, a. 3). At this point the terminology of the vows is established.

Ambiguity of Meaning[2]

It is not often that the same word can point to one of the world's great evils and to one of the highest aspirations of the human spirit. Poverty is one such word. While we may at times regret its inherent ambiguity we can also accept it as a challenge forcing us to delve more deeply into the meanings we assign to the term. The poverty that prevents millions of people throughout the world from living a fully human life is clearly evil and needs to be eradicated. This poverty deprives its victims of adequate nourishment, housing, medical care and educational opportunities. It makes sheer survival a daily struggle and human flourishing an unrealisable dream. It challenges the affluent, the powerful and even the merely comfortable to ask what they are doing or can do to end this evil, this assault on human dignity. No one can claim to be committed to justice without working for the elimination of poverty.

It is easier to speak of poverty as an evil than as a good. Yet all the major religious traditions hold out poverty as (somewhat paradoxically) both a goal to be striven for and as the only pathway to that goal. They offer a variety of explanations for this teaching, explore the most helpful means to attain poverty, and confront with honesty the resistances that men and women experience to embracing this value in their lives. Yet however much these traditions have in common, each is distinct. Its understanding of poverty is situated within, and influenced by, a complex of philosophical, theological, religious and cultural convictions which colour and nuance its theory and practice. Our present reflections are taking place within the Judeo-Christian tradition, more specifically within that shared (for the most part) by Catholic and Orthodox Christians. These agree in positing poverty as an essential component of the religious life. However, before dealing with religious life as such, we need to explore the Scriptures, beginning with the Old Testament.

Wisdom Literature

Wealth, particularly in the Wisdom literature, was seen as a sign of divine generosity, a reward for fidelity to God, and part of that fullness of life that God promised to his elect. It brought with it many advantageous consequences, including economic independence. This protected its beneficiaries from the need to beg or from enslavement to creditors. It could even make it possible to win highly-placed and influential friends. Furthermore, the acquisition of wealth presupposed admirable human qualities such as an entrepreneurial spirit, a willingness to work hard and sound practical judgement, as well as determination, persistence and courage.

Yet in spite of all these positive features the Wisdom writers judged wealth to be a good of the second order. Of higher importance were other less tangible blessings, such as peace of soul, a blameless reputation, health, virtue and wisdom. No one, they taught, can buy love or procure an exemption from death. Moreover, not all wealth came from God. There was ill-gotten wealth, which would only lead its owner to disaster. Above all, it is difficult for a person to remain faithful to God in prosperity because easy living desiccates and shrivels the heart. Rich and powerful individuals can be seduced by wealth into thinking that they can ignore God. Anyone who goes down this path is not only a sinner but a fool!

All of this complexity and ambiguity around wealth (its goodness and its dangers) led the Wisdom writers to opt for a golden mean. This is proposed in a prayer such as we might imagine as coming from one of the Greek philosophers:

> Give me neither poverty nor riches;
> Feed me with the food that I need,
> Or I shall be full, and deny you,
> And say, 'Who is the Lord?'
> Or I shall be poor, and steal,
> And profane the name of my God. (Prov 30:8–9)

The Prophets and the Anawim

The gap between the rich and the poor in Israel became most marked during the period of the monarchy. Wealth became concentrated in the hands of the king and his court. In an increasingly bureaucratic society government was often corrupt and its taxation of citizens unjust. Landowners alone enjoyed civil rights and judges were appointed from their number. As a result justice was compromised. Against this background two developments occurred: the strictures of the prophets against those who ground down the poor, and the emergence of what came to be known as the spirituality of the *anawim*, the poor of Yahweh. These developments were linked.

The prophets raised and addressed some difficult questions. Why did God allow this great disparity between rich and poor? Or appear to condone the injustice that undergirded it? The prophets became fervent advocates for the poor and severe critics of their oppressors. But they went further, declaring that the poor were protected by God and that one day God would come and give them justice. They even claimed that the poor were the chosen ones of God and were specially loved by him. This was radical and subversive teaching.

However, the word 'poverty' gradually came to mean more than simply deprivation, penury and oppression. It could also imply a religious disposition: one that was meek, humble, gentle, peaceful and utterly dependent on God. The poor, the *anawim*, were the little ones, the powerless who had no influential protectors to fight or plead on their behalf. But they waited patiently for God, who alone would vindicate them. They relied on God absolutely and were confident that he would be true to his promises.

Life of Jesus

The spirituality of the *anawim* carried over into the New Testament. It can be seen throughout the Infancy Narratives in figures such as Zechariah and Elizabeth, Mary and Joseph, Simeon and Anna. The Magnificat has been called an *anawim* psalm that beautifully articulates this spirituality. Mary prays:

> God's mercy is for those who fear him
> From generation to generation.
> He has shown strength with his arm;
> He has scattered the proud in the thoughts of their hearts.
> He has brought down the powerful from their thrones,
> And lifted up the lowly;
> He has filled the hungry with good things,
> And sent the rich away empty. (Lk 2:50–53)

The evocative words and images of the Magnificat illuminate the religious culture into which Jesus was born and in which he was raised. His poverty, grounded in a willing acceptance of his humanity and its limitations, engendered a total dependence on the one he called his Abba, his dear Father. Out of this *anawim* spirituality came his deter-

25

mination to be baptised by his cousin John in the Jordan. There he associated himself with the multitude of people who thronged around, confessing their sins and pleading for God's mercy.

On entering into his public ministry, Jesus continued to express this spirituality by a series of significant decisions. Some affected his lifestyle: 'The Son of Man has nowhere to lay his head'. (Mt 8:20) Others delineated his mission: 'To bring good news to the poor ... to proclaim release to the captives ... recovery of sight to the blind ... to let the oppressed go free'. (Lk 4:18) As his ministry evolved over time, Jesus' habit of associating with those on the margins of Jewish society scandalised the sanctimonious elite and drew their ire.

> When the scribes of the Pharisees saw that he was eating with sinners and tax collectors, they said to his disciples, 'Why does he eat with tax collectors and sinners?' When Jesus heard this, he said to them, 'Those who are well have no need of a physician, but those who are sick; I have come to call not the righteous but sinners'. (Mk 2:16–17)

Eventually this criticism, along with other charges, morphed into threats against his life and later into his arrest and trial. During his Passion, in spite of being tempted to abandon his *anawim* spirituality, Jesus delved into its depths all the more resolutely. He endured a series of excruciating diminishments which brought him to nadirs of helplessness and into a dark night in which he felt abandoned even by his Father. Yet he continued to trust and maintained an inner freedom that enabled him, as he took his last breath, to hand over his spirit into the care of that same Father, his Abba. (Lk 23:46) This was to be the ultimate expression of his poverty.

Later, after the Resurrection and the coming of the Spirit at Pentecost, Jesus' followers interpreted what they had seen through the lens of the Suffering Servant texts in Isaiah. They found the fulfilment of these prophecies most obviously in the Passion, but they also read them back (as it were) into the public life. This occurred especially when they were reminiscing on Jesus' healing ministry, as, for example, in two texts in Matthew:

> That evening they brought to him many who were possessed with demons, and he cast out the spirits with a word, and cured all who were sick. This was to fulfil what had been spoken through the prophet Isaiah: 'He took our infirmities and bore our diseases'. (Mt 8:16–17)

And after later healings we read:

> This was to fulfil what had been spoken through the prophet Isaiah,
> 'Here is my servant, whom I have chosen,
> My beloved, with whom my soul is well pleased.
> I will put my Spirit upon him,
> And he will proclaim justice to the Gentiles.
> He will not wrangle or cry aloud,
> Nor will anyone hear his voice in the streets.
> He will not break a bruised reed
> Or quench a smouldering wick
> Until he brings justice to victory.
> And in his name the Gentiles will hope'. (Mt 12:15–21)

Teaching of Jesus

In his teaching Jesus consistently praised the *anawim*, such as the woman suffering from apparently incurable haemorrhages who approached him with great faith in his power to heal (Mt 9:20–22), or the poor widow who generously put her few remaining coins into the Temple treasury. (Mk 12:41–44) Furthermore, Jesus declared blessed both those who were materially poor (Lk 6:20) and those who were poor in spirit. (Mt 5:3) This has led to endless and sometimes angst-

filled questioning (not least among religious) as to the relationship between material and spiritual poverty. There is sometimes a tendency
(or a self-serving desire?) to keep them separate, most boldly by pro-
posing that poverty of spirit can be attained without any reference to
material poverty. This is a difficult stance to maintain in light of the
scriptural evidence.

There is no doubt that Jesus called some (at least) to material or
actual poverty. He said to the well-intentioned but rich ruler (who had
observed all the commandments from his youth): 'There is still one
thing lacking. Sell all that you own and distribute the money to the
poor, and you will have treasure in heaven; then come, follow me'. (Lk
18:22) The ruler, however, reacted with shock and grief. Seeing this
Jesus commented:

> How hard it is for those who have wealth to enter the
> kingdom of God! Indeed, it is easier for a camel to go
> through the eye of a needle than for someone who is
> rich to enter the kingdom of God. (Lk 18:24–25)

In his response to the ruler Jesus had actually gone further than pro-
posing that he live according to the *anawim* tradition. He adopted a
more radical approach to material poverty by raising the possibility of
its becoming a voluntary choice, not simply a burden to be accepted.
Inevitably the impulsive Peter intervened:

> Then Peter said, 'Look, we have left our homes and fol-
> lowed you'. And he said to them, 'Truly I tell you, there
> is no one who has left house or wife or brothers or par-
> ents or children, for the sake of the kingdom of God,
> who will not get back very much more in this age, and
> in the age to come eternal life'. (Lk 18:28–30)

Elsewhere Jesus insisted on making material poverty a condition of
the apostolate. He sent out his seventy disciples with the words: 'Go
on your way. See, I am sending you out like lambs into the midst of

wolves. Carry no purse, no bag, no sandals; and greet no one on the road'. (Lk 10:3–4) It is as if the effectiveness of the Good News is dependent on the poor lifestyle of those who proclaim it. Poverty lends credibility to the message.

Acts and Paul

The New Testament has, of course, much more to say about poverty. The early Church in Jerusalem devised its own way of making it central to its communal life. Two short summary passages at the end of Acts 2 and 4 remain an archetype and set a standard for Christians in any age. The latter text reads:

> Now the whole group of those who believed were of one heart and soul, and no one claimed private ownership of any possessions, but everything they owned was held in common ... There was not a needy person among them, for as many as owned lands or houses sold them and brought the proceeds of what was sold. They laid it at the apostles' feet, and it was distributed to each as any had need. (Acts 4:32–37)

These summary passages may be somewhat idealised. Nevertheless, they paint a vivid picture of what the Jerusalem Church saw as the way of life that would best give expression to their following of the poor and compassionate Jesus. Notice how they put the economically poor and needy at the centre of their concern, and also how this way of living poverty is necessarily communal. It only works if there is already a vibrant sense of the Church as a community, and of the members being 'of one heart and soul'. These texts challenge today's Church to rectify its deficiencies in growing into a world-wide *communio* rather than a more or less well-run bureaucratic organisation.

Paul frequently alluded to one or other aspect of poverty, which had become an important part of his witness and preaching. He did not promote poverty as a good or a goal in itself, but portrayed it as woven into his experience of ministry.

> Not that I am referring to being in need, for I have learned to be content with whatever I have. I know what it is to have little, and I know what it is to have plenty. In any and all circumstances I have learned the secret of being well-fed and of going hungry, of having plenty and of being in need. I can do all things through him who strengthens me. (Phil 4:11–13)

Elsewhere he touched on what we now call gratuity of ministries. This is a point we will need to revisit in the next chapter. Paul wrote:

> If I proclaim the gospel, this gives me no ground for boasting, for an obligation is laid on me, and woe to me if I do not proclaim the gospel. For if I do this of my own will, I have a reward; but if not of my own will, I am entrusted with a commission. What then is my reward? Just this: that in my proclamation I may make the gospel free of charge, so as not to make full use of my rights in the gospel. (1 Cor 9:16–18)[3]

The above quotes from Paul dealt with the practicalities and the ministerial effectiveness of poverty. But he sometimes moved from *praxis* to *theoria*. Most of all, his hymn acclaiming the double *kenosis* or self-emptying of Christ unveiled poverty in its deepest theological meaning. It is true that the actual word 'poverty' does not appear, but *kenosis* or self-emptying becomes its synonym.

> Let the same mind be in you that was in Christ Jesus,
> Who, though he was in the form of God,
> Did not regard equality with God as something to be exploited,
> But emptied himself, taking the form of a slave,
> Being born in human likeness.
> And being found in human form,

He humbled himself and became obedient to the point of
   death –
Even death on a cross. (Phil 2:5–8)

The following verses (9–11) celebrate the exaltation of Christ which
is the Father's response to the Son's *kenosis*. All Christians share in
both of these 'movements'. After a lifetime of self-emptying in love
and service of others, they descend into the ultimate poverty of the
grave and are raised again with Christ to a new, fuller and everlasting
life.

Paul expressed something of this same theological insight in a simpler way in 2 Corinthians, but now using the word 'poverty'. 'For you
know the generous act of our Lord Jesus Christ, that though he was
rich, yet for your sakes he became poor, so that by his poverty you
might become rich'. (2 Cor 8:9)

Beginnings of Religious Life

In spite of this abundance of biblical teaching, the men and wom-
en who went out into the desert in such remarkable numbers from
the second century onwards still had to discover how poverty was to
be lived there. How could they express and structure poverty in the
circumstances of their newly emerging anchoritic or coenobitic life?
Their struggles to implement an authentic Christian poverty became
a major part of their discernment and of what we have referred to as
'the wisdom of the desert'.

For John Cassian (c.365–435), the enthusiastic promotor of desert
monasticism in Gaul, poverty had to be manifest from the very beginning of a monk's life. Before being allowed to enter the monastery the
applicant must spend 10 days or more lying on the ground outside its
door in an attitude of needy supplication.

And when he has embraced the knees of all the brothers passing by and has been purposely rebuked and

> disdained by everyone ... and has been visited with
> numerous insults and reproaches ... when the ardour
> of his intention has been proven and he has thus been
> received, he is asked with the utmost earnestness if, from
> his former possessions, the contamination of even a sin-
> gle copper coin clings to him. (*Institutes*, 4.3.1)[4]

And as the monk has begun in utter poverty, so must he remain steadfast in it throughout his entire life. 'You must abide until the end in the poverty *(nuditas)* that you professed before God and his angels' (*Institutes* 4.36.2).[5] Needless to say, Cassian regarded the renunciation of material goods as inherently linked with the renunciations of sexual pleasure and of one's own will (chastity and obedience). All three were inseparable facets of the one renunciation – that of the self. From this flowed 'purity of heart', which he saw as the goal of monastic life.

CHAPTER 3

Religious Poverty: a Synthesis of Values

Evolution of Poverty

The harsh poverty of the desert that Cassian introduced into Gaul did not prevail universally. In the east the Rule of St Basil, and in the west the Rules of St Augustine and St Benedict, had a more lasting influence. With the arrival of the mendicants in the twelfth century monasticism ceased to be the only, or even the main, expression of religious life. This development was followed by the emergence of explicitly apostolic orders in the sixteenth and later centuries. In more modern times further variations of religious life, and more broadly of consecrated life, have appeared. Through all this evolution there has been a constant need to reinterpret the ideal of poverty in creative yet authentic ways in light of emerging charisms and shifting apostolic goals. Changing social, political and economic systems also require a rethinking of how best to realise this ideal. Yet it must be emphasised that no founder has ever set out to abolish poverty or even to diminish its importance. Furthermore, reform movements have mostly been built on a return to the primitive observance of poverty in a particular tradition.

This continuous development has been possible because poverty is not a clear-cut, unambiguous, clearly definable value that can only ever be lived out in one specific way. As an essential element in religious life, poverty is best understood as a combination or synthesis of values and attitudes that will be expressed through a range of structures and behaviours. In some rare instances actual, material poverty is the central, identifying element; the charism that gives a tradition its distinctiveness – the early Franciscan movement is an example. But in most cases this is not so. Especially in apostolic institutes, where the central, identifying element is mission, there is need for a flexibility and adaptability of structure and behaviour. This involves the relativising, but emphatically not the elimination, of the commitment to material poverty. Therein lies both the danger of ambivalence and the challenge to authenticity.

This chapter will outline the main expressions of poverty that have consistently been present in the history of religious life. None of them can ever be disregarded completely, but the emphasis on each will vary according to different times, places and cultures and, above all, according to specific charisms. These sundry expressions of poverty all witness to a way of life that is God-centred, Christ-centred and other-centred rather than self-centred. They are all forms of *kenosis*.

Characteristics of the Synthesis

No personal ownership of material goods
In some ways the renunciation of *proprietas* is the bedrock of the profession of poverty. We have already seen instances of this teaching in the Desert tradition. Francis of Assisi opened Chapter 1 of the Earlier Rule[1] of his friars with this assertion:

> The rule and life of these brothers is this: to live in obe-

dience, in chastity, and without anything of their own,
and to follow the teaching and the footprints of our
Lord Jesus Christ.[2]

Here, what we call poverty is represented simply by the phrase
'without anything of their own', *sine proprio*. Of course, if we accept
that poverty is, in fact, a complex of values, the renunciation of personal ownership will be just one of them. Nevertheless, it is significant
that Francis in his day was satisfied to allow this formula, *sine proprio*,
to stand for the whole synthesis. This is one factor in naming it 'the
bedrock of the profession of poverty'. Later, in Chapter 8 of the Earlier Rule, Francis wrote:

> Therefore, let us who have left all things behind take
> care that we do not lose the kingdom of heaven for so
> little. And if we were to find coins in any place, let us
> give them no more thought than the dust which we
> crush with our feet; for all [this is] *vanity of vanities, and
> all is vanity.* And if by chance – which God forbid – it
> should happen that some brother has collected or is
> hoarding money or coins, with the sole exception of the
> needs of the sick as mentioned above, all the brothers
> are to consider him as a false brother and an apostate,
> and a thief and a robber, and as the one who held the
> purse [Judas] unless he has truly repented.[3]

This trenchant statement echoes Cassian's strictures on 'the con-
tamination of even a single copper'.

Religious call nothing their own ('mine') but undertake to be dependent for their material needs on the community and ultimately
on God. This commitment both gives expression to and facilitates an
inner detachment. Wealth, while innately good because part of the
abundance of God's creation, is seen as capable of having pernicious
side-effects on its possessors. For example:

35

(a) It may induce them to extravagance and indulgence.

(b) It has the effect of separating and alienating people from one another.

(c) It easily leads to self-sufficiency, arrogance and, ultimately, pride.

On the other hand the spiritual benefits that result from a commitment to live *sine proprio* are both personal (the delight of inner freedom) and communal (solidarity with others, especially the poor and needy). This freely undertaken rejection of all that one could legitimately own and enjoy is symbolic of all the other renunciations that are envisaged as accompanying it, or arising from it.

Possession of goods in common

Complementing the absence of personal ownership, its other face, as it were, is the possession of goods in common. This lifestyle is legitimately called communistic, and is based on the practice of the early Christians in Jerusalem. (Acts 2:42–47; 4:32–37)[4] The possession of goods in common constitutes a core value of this community but it is good to situate it in the context of their life as a whole. These Christians are presented in Acts as:

(a) A community of believers formed by the proactive presence of the Holy Spirit;

(b) Constantly deepening their knowledge of the apostles' teaching;

(c) Committed to each other, and especially to the poor, through a thoroughgoing sharing of goods;

(d) Symbolising and celebrating their union through the table-fellowship that is the Eucharist;

(e) Worshipping God through the practice of personal, communal and liturgical prayer;

(f) Witnessing to the Risen Lord through their power of healing and the eloquence of their mutual loving.

Possession of goods in common, therefore, can be seen as a sacramental expression of the sharing of their life of faith. This linkage between levels of sharing is also made in an early second-century text, the *Didache* or *Teaching of the Twelve Apostles*:

> Do not turn away from the needy; rather, share everything with your brother, and do not say: 'It is private property'. If you are sharers in what is imperishable, how much more so in the things that perish![5]

A simple lifestyle

The standard of poverty suggested by the adjective 'simple' (as we understand the word today) would not have been sufficiently rigorous for Cassian's monks or Francis' friars. But it may be what is required of those whose material poverty has legitimately been relativised (especially by the demands of mission). Other adjectives that might be appropriate to such a lifestyle include modest, frugal or unpretentious. They all point to a way of living that entails thriftiness or economy in the use of money. It approximates the prudent way in which a family of slender means learns to conserve life's necessities.

Commitment to a simple lifestyle also raises many interrelated questions. Religious may ask themselves:

- ☛ Where do we live (in affluent or deprived areas of our cities and towns)?
- ☛ With whom do we identify and associate (the rich, the middle class or the poor)?
- ☛ Does anything in our lifestyle embarrass us (especially in the presence of the poor or marginalised)?
- ☛ Is our lifestyle a witness or a counter-witness to the Good News?
- ☛ Does our living of poverty match our rhetoric about poverty?

Put positively, when religious have a genuinely simple lifestyle, they offer the world (especially in the west) a counter-cultural critique. By deliberately rejecting the materialist and consumerist values of the dominant culture they are truly prophetic. Their witness also has an ecological significance, since a simple lifestyle contributes to the preservation of scarce and fast-dwindling natural resources. Pope Francis has said, with all the earth's inhabitants in mind:

> We need to take up an ancient lesson, found in different religious traditions and also in the Bible. It is the conviction that 'less is more'. A constant flood of new consumer goods can baffle the heart and prevent us from cherishing each thing and each moment … Christian spirituality proposes a growth marked by moderation and the capacity to be happy with little. It is a return to that simplicity which allows us to stop and appreciate the small things, to be grateful for the opportunities which life affords us, to be spiritually detached from what we possess, and not to succumb to sadness for what we lack.[6]

Hospitality

The author of the Letter to the Hebrews wrote: 'Do not neglect to show hospitality to strangers, for by doing that some have entertained angels without knowing it'. (Heb 13:2) Hospitality is a virtue that expresses a community's desire and determination to reach out to and include others from beyond its own ranks. What religious share with each other (through possession of goods in common), they do not cling to in a form of corporate selfishness or even avarice. A community, as much as an individual, can become self-absorbed, even narcissistic, and this can lead to a kind of isolationist mentality. But a spiritually healthy community will wish to be an open, accepting, wel-

coming group of Christians, followers of the always welcoming Jesus.[7]
Such a community will wish to share, not only its food and drink, but
also its members' own lived experience of acceptance, warmth, love
and faith.

It can also be helpful to consider hospitality as a form of almsgiving, but one that is inter-personal, communitarian, and not limited to
the material. It transcends the kind of quasi-anonymous giving that
happens when we send a donation to some good cause by cheque
or electronic transfer. Furthermore, the meaning of hospitality (and
almsgiving) can be broadened out to include, for example, the care of
the unwell and the offering of a listening ear to the disturbed.

But, as with their commitment to a simple lifestyle, it is good
for religious to ask some potentially awkward questions about
their practice of hospitality – its quality and its inclusiveness. For
example:

- ☛ Whom do we invite into our houses (and so into our lives)?
- ☛ Do we maintain an open door only to our friends and those
  we find congenial?
- ☛ Do we welcome the 'tax collectors and sinners' of today?
- ☛ Who, for us, is the 'stranger', the 'other', who may well be
  an angel in disguise?

With that last question we are engaging with the mystical aspect of
hospitality. The tradition requires that we see Christ in every guest,
and especially in every poor guest. We find this ideal in the moving
53rd chapter of the Rule of St Benedict.

> Guests should always be treated with respect and defer-
> ence. Those attending them both on arrival and depar-
> ture should show this by a bow of the head or even a full
> prostration on the ground, which will leave no doubt
> that it is indeed Christ who is received and venerated
> in them.[8]

A life of work

The authenticity of a simple lifestyle is demonstrated when it has work as one of its central components. Such work is not to be confused with the dilettantism of the rich and leisured; an option rather than a necessity. As with the apostle Paul, the labours undertaken by religious are mostly related to their ministries. But, again like Paul, religious may also work, whenever necessary, to earn their living and not become a burden on others. Work of either kind displays a concrete, visible and real identification with the common lot of humankind. One might argue that (all other things being equal) the more such work is carried out shoulder to shoulder with others the clearer is its witness value. That strange, troubled, yet brilliant Frenchwoman, Simone Weil, wrote:

> Nothing gives me more pain than the idea of separating
> myself from the immense and unfortunate multitude of
> unbelievers. I have the essential need, and I think I can
> say the vocation, to move among men [*sic*] of every class
> and complexion, mixing with them and sharing their life
> and outlook, so far, that is to say, as conscience allows.[9]

Simone identified herself with the post-Christian working-class people of France, yet she remained intriguingly different from them.

Religious also bring something different to the environments in which they toil; they bring the Good News. They witness to an approach to work that does not regard it as a curse on the human race (a false biblical interpretation), nor as a commodity to be sold in the marketplace (a destructive capitalist interpretation). Instead they see it, and invite others to see it, as

    (a) An expression of human dignity;

    (b) A manifestation of human solidarity and interdependence;

    (c) A sharing in God's ongoing act of creation;

    (d) An exercise in stewardship of the earth.

Gratuity of ministries

This is probably the aspect of religious poverty that is most difficult to implement in many parts of the world today. Economic necessity often forces religious to ask for payments or stipends for their ministries. This may be the only way to keep institutions open or to enable individual religious to contribute to the upkeep of their community. It is not an ideal situation, and many religious feel uneasy and even resistant to putting a financial value on their ministries. Such feelings are by no means unhealthy. Religious should always at least *desire* to offer their services freely, without any thought of recompense or remuneration. The words of Jesus still ring out clearly: 'You received without payment; give without payment'. (Mt 10:8)

Undertaking some voluntary work in addition to one's paid work can be one way of ensuring a certain 'balance'. But not all religious can do this without endangering their health. Hospitality is another way of offering something freely to others. We saw above how authentic and multi-layered an expression of poverty this can be. Yet, for all the good intentions among most religious, questions remain. Among the most unsettling is the one that asks: 'Who are discriminated against (disadvantaged, excluded, turned away) when our ministries are not gratuitous?' The answer is self-evident: 'Those who are most in need'! This uncomfortable conclusion leads smoothly into the next topic.

Preferential option for the poor

This phrase evokes the attitude of Yahweh in the Old Testament and of Jesus in the gospels. It is now official teaching in the Church that all Christians are called to make the same preferential option.[10] Or, as Pope Francis put it in strikingly personal terms, 'I want a Church which is poor and for the poor'.[11] It is, therefore, obvious that religious are not singular in being called to this particular demonstration of poverty. Nevertheless, since they are by profession evangelically poor (poor by choice), there is a particular exigency on them to be in solidarity with those who are economically, socially and educationally poor (those who are poor by circumstance). This preferential option is lived out on a spectrum that, under grace, is capable of developing an inner momentum. Such a spectrum might look like this:

(a) Compassionate and prayerful benevolence towards individuals or communities in any form of distress;

(b) Remedial care and accompaniment of such individuals or communities;

(c) Conscientization or the sensitising both of the poor themselves and of their oppressors to the reality of the injustice being perpetrated against/by them;

(d) Undertaking an active role in the struggle to dismantle unjust social structures, replacing them with structures that will respect and enhance human dignity.

Two relatively new terms in today's justice vocabulary are 'ecology' and 'advocacy'. Pope Francis has argued that, among the many reasons to be involved with environmental issues, one of the most powerful is that the degradation of nature impacts most heavily on the world's poor. Hence, lack of concern for the environment equals lack of concern for the poor.

> The human environment and the natural environment deteriorate together; we cannot adequately combat environmental degradation unless we attend to causes related to human and social degradation. In fact, the deterioration of the environment and of society affects the most vulnerable people on the planet.[12]

Advocacy is another means of promoting justice that has opened up for many religious in recent years. We see it exemplified in efforts to halt the trafficking across political borders of the young and vulnerable (mostly women) for purposes of prostitution or other forms of slavery. But advocacy has a role to play in combatting *all* forms of injustice.

Dependence on providence

Once more we recall the spirit of the *anawim* and the faith, the loving trust in the Father, which Jesus calls for in the gospels. While this is essentially an inner attitude of the heart, it still needs to be validated externally (or, in other words, 'incarnated') in a person's or a community's way of life. In particular it needs to influence the way of making decisions. Do religious use as a foundational criterion the teaching of Jesus as he points to the birds of the air and the lilies of the field? (Lk 12:22–31) Does their decision-making exhibit a willingness to take risks, especially in embarking on bold apostolic enterprises? Many founders of religious orders and congregations have exhibited such a willingness, trusting implicitly that 'the Lord will provide'. Such a prophetic proclamation (for that is what it is) is currently counter-cultural and, as a result, particularly difficult to make. We live in a risk-averse and safety-obsessed society. Perhaps religious need to cry out: 'I believe; help my unbelief!' (Mk 9:24)

Union with the poor Christ

The ultimate motivation and inspiration for evangelical poverty is the desire for union with the poor and suffering Christ. This is one aspect of our synthesis that cannot be relativized. Without this mystical underpinning poverty (however sincerely practised) is only asceticism, mortification, self-denial, philosophical ideology or a functional contribution to mission. But those who best represent the Christian religious tradition keep returning to the figure of Christ, poor, despised, betrayed, suffering and dying.

In the Second Letter of St Clare to Blessed Agnes of Prague, she encourages her friend in these words:

> But as a poor virgin, embrace the poor Christ. Look
> upon him who became contemptible for you, and fol-
> low him, making yourself contemptible in the world for
> him. Your spouse, though more beautiful than the chil-
> dren of men, despised, struck, scourged untold times
> throughout his whole body, and then died amid the suf-
> ferings of the Cross. O most noble Queen, gaze upon
> him, consider him, contemplate him, as you desire to
> imitate him.[13]

Those familiar with the Spiritual Exercises will remember the
prayer proposed by St Ignatius Loyola when presenting 'The Third
Way of Being Humble':

> In order to imitate Christ our Lord better and to be
> more like him here and now, I desire and choose pover-
> ty with Christ poor rather than wealth; contempt with
> Christ laden with it rather than honours. Even further,
> I desire to be regarded as a useless fool for Christ, who
> before me was regarded as such, rather than as a wise or
> prudent person in this world.[14]

Finally, from the Jesuit Constitutions there is an imaginative and
vibrant passage which, in many ways, sums up the ideal of religious
poverty (even if the word itself does not appear):

> It is likewise very important to bring to the attention of
> those who are being examined, emphasising it and giv-
> ing it great weight in the sight of our Creator and Lord,
> to how great a degree it helps and profits in the spiritu-
> al life to abhor in its totality and not in part whatever
> the world loves and embraces, and to accept and desire
> with all possible energy whatever Christ our Lord has
> loved and embraced. Just as the men of the world who

follow the world love and seek with such great diligence honours, fame, and esteem for a great name on earth, as the world teaches them, so those who proceed spiritually and truly follow Christ our Lord love and intensely desire everything opposite. That is to say, they desire to clothe themselves with the same garb and uniform of their Lord because of the love and reverence owed to him, to such an extent that where there would be no offence to his Divine Majesty and no imputation of sin to the neighbour, they desire to suffer injuries, false accusations, and affronts, and to be held and esteemed as fools (but without their giving any occasion for this), because of their desire to resemble and imitate in some manner our Creator and Lord Jesus Christ, by putting on his garb and uniform, since it was for our spiritual profit that he clothed himself as he did. For he gave us an example that in all things possible to us we might seem, with the aid of his grace, to imitate and follow him, since he is the way that leads to life.[15]

CHAPTER 4

Biblical Wisdom Behind Chastity

Human Freedom

The mystery of human freedom and human choice fascinates, energises and disturbs us at one and the same time. This is especially so when the road a person chooses is 'the one less travelled by', a minority (if not a singular) choice. Then the mystery deepens. What made Robert Frost choose the way of artistic integrity as a poet rather than some easier, more ordinary, more secure path in life? What vision stimulates those who live on the frontiers of the human condition, giving them an insatiable urge to bring about 'a new creation' in the fields of art, literature, music, science or politics? What brings about a radical transformation in Christians who are 'born again'? What leads some Christians to make a lifelong commitment to serve God through vows of poverty, chastity and obedience? These examples of minority choices are all, at least in a broad sense, prophetic. They raise questions about ultimate meaning, values to live by, ideals to aspire to, and the possibilities of transcendence. Such questions challenge not only individuals but society as a whole.

In the case of religious, who have made one specific kind of minority choice, their vowed chastity raises the most obvious issues in
today's sex-obsessed culture. Most of these issues surface from time to
time, even painfully, among religious themselves. To be counter-cultural does not immunise a person against the pervasive influence of
the dominant culture. Few religious are free from the nagging doubts
about chastity that can arise no matter how long they have been in
religious life. For most, these doubts tend to come and go, depending
on the evolution of their human relationships and other changing
circumstances in their lives. They constitute a crisis and need to be
addressed. But they are not necessarily a threat to a person's commitment to chastity. In fact, most such crises lead eventually to a recom-
mitment to the vow of chastity, but now with greater awareness and
realism -- and at a deeper level than before.

Old Testament

We do not often turn to the Jewish tradition in our search for the
meaning of consecrated celibacy. We tend to think of that tradition
as providing no insights into celibacy as a religious value. On the con-
trary, Jewish writing, whether the Old Testament or rabbinical literature, is regarded as providing strong arguments *against* living a celibate
life rather than *for* living it. By and large this is a correct interpretation. Yet there are two reasons at least why an exploration of this
tradition is worthwhile. Firstly, the very force of its arguments against
celibacy helps us to understand how Jesus' own choice not to marry
was so radical and counter-cultural. Secondly, a closer look at some
of this literature reveals a gradual, tentative development, a sporadic
admission that celibacy might be a legitimate religious choice in certain specific circumstances.[1]

In the Old Testament virginity in women prior to marriage was
mandatory and esteemed. But the idea of virginity as a state of life is,

in the main, foreign to Israel's religious culture. The foundational text is found in the Creation narrative.

> So God created humankind in his image,
> in the image of God he created them;
> male and female he created them.
>
> God blessed them, and God said to them, 'Be fruitful and multiply, and fill the earth and subdue it; and have dominion over the fish of the sea and over the birds of the air and over every living thing that moves upon the earth'. (Gen 1:27–28)

The key phrase here is, 'Be fruitful and multiply'. Originally this was interpreted as God's blessing on the human race as a whole, guaranteeing its fecundity and continuity. But over time 'Be fruitful and multiply' came to be interpreted as a command that applied to every single Israelite. This was especially so in rabbinical teaching. As a result of this change of meaning from blessing to command, a fruitful marriage became a religious and social imperative. Consequently, a woman's childlessness was considered by others, and felt by herself, to be shameful.

This reality lies behind the bitter sibling rivalry between the barren Rachel and her sister Leah, who had borne their husband Jacob four sons.

> When Rachel saw that she bore Jacob no children, she envied her sister; and she said to Jacob, 'Give me children or I shall die'. Jacob became very angry with Rachel and said, 'Am I in the place of God, who has withheld from you the fruit of the womb?' (Gen 30:1–2)

An even more dramatic example is the story of the daughter of Jephthah, a military leader among the Israelites. He had made a rash vow, that if God granted him victory over the Ammonites, he would sacrifice the first living creature he met on his return home.

This turned out to be his daughter, an only child. Knowing her fate, the girl expressed a last wish, which was to be allowed to go into the mountains for two months with her women friends. This was to be an opportunity, she said, 'to bewail my virginity'. She did not want to grieve for her imminent death (this she could accept with equanimity) but to lament that she had to die *while still a virgin*. (Jg 11:34–40) This appalling prospect was breaking her heart.

Throughout the Old Testament there are only two cases of someone renouncing marriage or being told by God to do so. The first involves the prophet Jeremiah.

> The word of the Lord came to me: You shall not take a wife, nor shall you have sons or daughters in this place. For thus says the Lord concerning the sons and daughters who are born in this place, and concerning the mothers who bear them and the fathers who beget them in this land. They shall not be lamented, nor shall they be buried; they shall become like dung on the surface of the ground. They shall perish by the sword and by famine, and their dead bodies shall become food for the birds of the air and for the wild animals of the earth. (Jer 16:1–4)

The symbolic gesture of Jeremiah's celibacy, his repudiation of marriage and fatherhood, were to be a sign of the calamities that God was about to send on the people: death through epidemics, famine, starvation and wars. Thus celibacy is identified with death, whereas life would be symbolised by marriage and fertility. A stark contrast indeed!

The second example is less straightforward and its interpretation somewhat tentative. Judith was a warrior who defended her people against their enemies. She was married to Manasseh but was apparently childless. After the death of her husband Judith received many

offers of marriage. She turned them all down. (Jud 16:21–22) This renouncing of a second marriage seems to have been due to her fidelity
to Manasseh, a fidelity that outlasted death and was stronger than her
desire to have children. Judith's heart was still with Manasseh. This
human reality trumped the requirements of the Jewish tradition. The
Book of Judith was written somewhere between the middle and end
of the second century BCE. The story suggests that during the two
centuries before Jesus there were occasional chinks in the dominant
mentality that was totally opposed to celibacy.

Rabbinic Tradition

In rabbinic teaching the fruitfulness of the human couple was linked
with the creative activity of God. Man and woman were most fully in
the image of God when in the act of procreation. Therefore, whoever
does not engage in that fruitful act, and so does not contribute to the
propagation of the race, diminishes the divine image in him or herself. (Gen 1:21, 9:7) This is a beautiful and emotive theological reflection on God's ideal for marriage. A harsher viewpoint is expressed in
another rabbinic saying: 'He who does not contribute to propagation
is like a man who sheds blood.' In other words, not to bring children
into the world is equivalent to killing those children. Even though this
is clearly an intemperate statement, the rabbis are, by and large, in
harmony with the outlook of the Old Testament.

However, there are again exceptions. Some narratives show that
it was permissible for a rabbi to separate himself from his wife, for
a limited time and with her consent, *in order to dedicate himself entirely
to the study of Torah.* This temporary celibacy within a marriage was
not unknown to Paul in later times, who approved of it under certain
conditions. (1 Cor 7:5) What is most important here is the motivation:
in order to dedicate himself entirely to the study of Torah. This study of Torah
is not just an academic exercise, a fulfilling of a rabbi's professional

obligation. Torah is one of the ways in which God is present among the Jewish people. It is sometimes identified with personified Wisdom. Its study, therefore, is a way of giving oneself to prayer, even to contemplation. It is a means of entering into union with God.

Finally we meet Rabbi Shimon ben Ahaz. He provides the only example of a rabbi who refrained permanently from entering into marriage. When other rabbis reproached him for this he replied: 'My soul is entirely taken up by Torah, and I have not time for marriage. Let the world be kept going by others!' A blunt affirmation certainly, but apposite to our investigation. In these remarkable exceptions within the rabbinic tradition, certain resonances with the Christian understanding of celibacy begin to be heard, hinting at what was to come.[2]

The Essenes

The Essenes were a sect within Judaism whose origins are placed around the period of the Maccabean wars. In the New Testament period they had gathered as a community at Qumran by the Dead Sea. They believed that they were living in the 'end-times', and out of this belief grew the practice of celibacy among some of their members. If the world is about to end, why propagate the race? This is referred to as an eschatological motivation. The Essenes expressed their ideas in two principal works. *The Manual of Discipline* seems to envisage a community comprised only of men. *The Rule of the Congregation*, however, refers to women and children, as well as laying down rules for sexual behaviour. It would seem, therefore, that the sect embraced both married and celibate members. John the Baptist almost certainly had links with the Essenes and may have lived among them for some time. Jesus was at least aware of their existence and may have known some of their adherents. It is unclear if there was any mutual influence.

Jesus

Lumen Gentium, the Vatican II document on the Church, teaches that

> Again, the religious state offers a closer imitation and an
> abiding representation in the church of the way of life
> that the Son of God made his own when he came into
> the world to do the will of the Father and which he put
> before the disciples who followed him (44).[3]

This representation (re-enactment?) of the way of life *(forma vitae)* chosen by Jesus for himself is the particular configuration of discipleship to which religious feel themselves called. For apostolic religious in particular, the primary model of their life-form is the adult Jesus in his public ministry. The term representation or re-enactment refers partly to the externals of his life, but predominantly to his inner motivations and values.

It has seldom been doubted that Jesus was celibate, although the gospels do not explicitly affirm it. But the arguments supporting his celibate state are compelling. His mother, along with his brothers and sisters (meaning either siblings or cousins) are specifically mentioned in the narrative of his public life. But there is never any reference to a wife or family of his own. His distinctive way of life is that of a person without ties, an itinerant healer and preacher, dedicated to proclaiming and establishing the Kingdom of God. His family, according to his own assertion, is composed of all those who do the will of the Father. (Mt12:48-50) But while the fact of Jesus' celibacy is evident enough, its genesis and motivation are less so. Hence we raise the question of choice: Did Jesus freely (in human terms) choose to remain celibate?

One theological tendency (a version of 'Christology from above') would link the celibacy of Jesus with his divinity. From this perspective his celibacy was the necessary corollary to his being Son of God. If any choice were involved it would be that made within the Trinity, not by Jesus in his humanity. He would have accepted his celibacy as a predetermined fact of life, just as were his Jewishness, his family of origin, his place and time of birth. While this view can be argued theologically, it sometimes masks psychological blocks to imagining Jesus as married, engaging in sexual intercourse and fathering human children.

An alternative approach (a version of 'Christology from below') takes the humanity of Jesus as its starting-point, and insists on his being 'one like us in all things except sin'. It opposes any hypothesis that would either dilute the fullness of human freedom enjoyed by Jesus or suggest that he was less than a fully sexual being. From this viewpoint the celibacy of Jesus had to be the result of a genuinely free choice (essentially no different from our own). It could have been made intuitively, or it could have been reached through experience, reflection and prayer (the process we call discernment). The bottom line is that it had to be *free*.

A Key Text

We turn now from Jesus' choice of celibacy for himself to his teaching on the subject. There are a number of gospel texts that are relevant, but we will concentrate on just one.

> 'And I say to you, whoever divorces his wife, except for unchastity, and marries another commits adultery.' His disciples said to him, 'If such is the case of a man with his wife, it is better not to marry.' But he said to them, 'Not everyone can accept this teaching, but only those to whom it is given. For there are eunuchs who have been so from birth, and there are eunuchs who have been made eunuchs by others, and there are eunuchs who have made themselves eunuchs for the sake of the kingdom of heaven. Let anyone accept this who can.'
> (Mt 19:9–12)

The context here is a discussion about divorce. Two rabbinic schools, those of Shammai and Hillel, held opposing views on the interpretation of Deuteronomy 24:1, which allowed for divorce in some circumstances. Jesus gives his support to neither school but instead teaches that marriage is indissoluble. He argues that the Mosaic bill of divorce did not imply God's approval, but was merely a reluctant toleration of existing customs in Israel. God's true will is to be found in the Creation narrative in Genesis. (1:27, 2:24) 'Therefore,' Jesus says, 'what God has joined together, let no one separate'. (Mt 19:6) The disciples are shocked at this severity, saying, 'If such is the case of a man with his wife, it is better not to marry.' Then Jesus goes even further. He takes up their words, 'it is better not to marry', and gives them a new and more radical meaning within the kingdom that he is inaugurating.

That is the common interpretation of the text. But it is possible that the original setting for Jesus' teaching at the end of this passage (v.12) was not that given in Matthew. These words may not have been addressed to the disciples in response to their problem with his teaching on marriage. Instead, his words may have been addressed to the Pharisees in response to their attacks on his celibate lifestyle. In this alternative scenario the term 'eunuch' was an insult thrown at Jesus in the same way that he was labelled 'glutton and a drunkard'. (Mt. 11:19) It was meant to express utter contempt and derision. To be a eunuch does not mean simply to be unmarried but to be *incapable of marriage*. Amazingly, Jesus accepts the term with all its grotesqueness, and then uses it to open up a new horizon. His words provide a motivation for celibacy, not simply as a choice not to marry, but as a choice to become incapable of marriage.

All this is based on a correlation between such celibacy and the kingdom. This correlation is not straightforward. The original Greek allows for two translations.[4] The one most frequently used reads: 'for the sake of the kingdom of heaven'. Here the kingdom is the end, while celibacy is a means to that end. This correlation can be further refined in terms of celibacy being a way of accessing the kingdom, or of serving the kingdom, or of establishing harmony between one's own life and the values of the kingdom. The kingdom, at least in its fullness, is a future reality for which the celibate is longing. In theological terminology this is an expression of a final eschatology.

The alternative translation reads: 'because of the kingdom'. Now the kingdom has already come, has already been experienced within, and this experience is precisely what grounds the decision to remain celibate. God has revealed himself, has broken into a person's life in such a captivating, irresistible manner that a commitment to celibacy becomes the only possible response. This is an example of a realised eschatology, where the reign of God is a present rather than a future reality.

A memorable expression of this understanding of consecrated celibacy, using easily recognisable biblical imagery, was given by the Dutch Dominican theologian, Edward Schillebeeckx.

> In view of their joy on finding the hidden pearl, some people cannot do otherwise than live unmarried. This religious experience itself makes them unmarriageable, actually incapable of marriage; their heart is where their treasure is.[5]

We might compare the case of a happily married woman or man who is existentially incapable of marrying anyone other than their beloved spouse.

Eschatology in Paul

For Paul, Christ's Church, in its inner reality, is carried forward by a powerful momentum towards the *eschaton* (the end) and the *pleroma* (the fullness of all things in Christ). Such a momentum, with its accompanying apocalyptic vision, relativizes all human values and institutions, including marriage. This eschatological drama forms the background for Paul's arguments in 1 Corinthians 7. He believes that Christians live in a world already transformed by the decisive saving event of Christ. This transformation will soon be consummated at the *parousia* (the second coming of Christ). At the time he wrote this letter, Paul seems to have presumed that this would happen in the lifetime of those he was addressing.

This is the reason why celibacy is a good and acceptable lifestyle 'in view of the impending crisis' (7:26). Those who marry 'will experience distress in this life' (7:28). 'The appointed time has grown short' (7:29). 'The present form of this world is passing away' (7:31). All these expressions have an eschatological connotation. So Paul's advice is that 'it is well for you to remain as you are' (7:26). Such a decision is legitimate since both marriage and celibacy are gifts from God (7:7). Consequently, the life-situation of Christians at the moment of baptism, when they consciously enter into the 'last days' or 'end times', is better not changed. Whether married or single, Christians can carry on the Lord's work for whatever (short) time remains (7:17, 21, 24, 27–31).

Paul's own personal preference for celibacy is clear: 'I wish that all were as I am myself' (7:7). He argues that the unmarried will have more freedom to exercise 'unhindered devotion to the Lord' (7:32–35). This points to their being fully involved in serving the community. The phrase about married persons having their interests divided is a pragmatic rather than a theological argument. Marriage, in itself, does not bring about a divided heart (between the Lord and one's spouse). However, marital and familial conflicts can sometimes arise from which Paul wishes people to be free.

The existential question for today's readers of 1 Corinthians 7 concerns the relevance (or irrelevance) of Paul's teaching for Christians who no longer expect the *parousia* to occur in their lifetime. Most believers, even the most committed, think about the *parousia* rarely, if at all. Still less do they attempt to understand it. One might ask: How aware are contemporary Christians of living in the 'end times'? How eagerly do they long for Christ to come in his glory? Is there any meeting point between their mentality and that of Paul?

The impression that 1 Corinthians 7 makes on religious (as distinct from Christians in general) is probably more oblique and allusive than direct and explicit. Most of the chapter's arguments do not apply to their situation. Even the single life spoken about by Paul is not the chastity (or consecrated celibacy) that religious profess. However, from the beginnings of religious life, there has always been present among its adherents a strong eschatological consciousness. It is largely this eschatological consciousness that gives religious life, and especially chastity, its prophetic character. The lives of religious witness to realities and values that are transcendent and that will not pass away with the dissolution of this present world. If religious were to lose this eschatological consciousness, or if it were to diminish to such an extent as to be imperceptible, their presence in the world would have become almost irrelevant. The light would have become dimmed and the salt would have lost its savour.

CHAPTER 5

Chastity and Human Maturity

From theology to lived experience

The preceding chapter mined the Hebrew and Christian scriptures for light on the choice, made freely by some Christians, to live in celibate chastity. These people are mostly, although not exclusively, to be found in religious life. It was a search for meaning and theological understanding. An exploration of the more explicitly human dimension of this life-form raises several questions. What is the lived experience of celibacy? How do religious relate to their embodied selves and to other embodied persons? Can they remain fully sexual human beings without repression, denial or other distortions? How do they interact with contemporary culture where to be sexually active (even outside marriage) is the norm? As religious struggle to be wholly authentic, the Church has helpful spiritual and moral guidance to offer. So also does the wisdom that is embedded in the traditions of their religious institutes. In more recent times the human sciences, especially the discipline of psychology, have provided their own valuable research-based expertise.

Let us begin by looking briefly at sexuality itself. How do we comprehend this multi-faceted and evolving concept in ways that are fresh rather than stale? Here I intend to be evocative rather than scientific. I propose that we try first to approach sexuality through Greco-Roman mythology, following to some degree the interpretation of Carl Jung. In particular I want to explore some of Jung's ideas about the archetypes. Those powerful inhabitants of the unconscious, ever-present but not always recognised, can be identified with the gods and goddesses of old.

Gods and Goddesses

A writer who has made use of Jung's teaching in this way is Jean Shinoda Bolen, a psychotherapist based in Berkeley, California. She became well-known internationally in the 1980s through two best-selling books, *Goddesses in Everywoman* and *Gods in Everyman*.[1] Bolen explored the influence of the gods and goddesses of ancient mythology on different types of human personality. Parallel in some ways to the Myers-Briggs Type Indicator or the Enneagram, Bolen enables us to delve into our inner dynamics through the stories of these gods and goddesses. She is, of course, identifying these mythological figures with the archetypes, and she does so in a positive and growth-oriented manner. My purpose in recalling these figures is more limited, and I will concentrate mostly on their potentially destructive effects.

Since the beginnings of Christianity there has often been expressed a nostalgia for the old pagan religion; for the gods and goddesses of nature – earthy, hot-blooded, passionate, full of uninhibited sexual energy. These gods and goddesses have existed in all cultures with their colourful, uncensored mythologies. In the western world we see this nostalgia showing itself in the rearguard resistance by the pagan Roman civilisation when Christianity was becoming the dominant religion of the empire. It surfaced again in medieval Europe in that era's widespread fascination with witchcraft and the occult. It even found expression during the Renaissance and the Reformation, neither of which movements was totally immune to its seductive power. In the late eighteenth and early nineteenth centuries this nostalgia re-emerged as a component of the Romantic Movement. In more recent times it is flourishing in aspects of what is sometimes known as neo-paganism, which is a multi-headed monster, not easily overcome. Among its more blatant manifestations was the Free Love ideology of the hippies in the 1960s. But its most virulent and toxic symptom in the twenty-first century is pornography, now universally and instantly available through the internet.

Nostalgia for What?

What then has been lost, or is perceived to have been lost, with the coming of Christianity that creates this peculiar yet powerful nostalgia? It is, above all else, the unconstrained enjoyment of sex. This is what the gods and goddesses offer us if only we would let go of our fear-fuelled inhibitions and scruples. Such insidiously seductive voices do not come only from outside of ourselves but also from within – from the goddesses in everywoman and the gods in everyman! Those who long for the ancient sexual licence of the pagan past regard Christianity as a religion of denial, of rejection, of inhibition, of weakness, of dread and, ultimately, of death. After all, Christianity's best-known symbol is that of a man awaiting death while he hangs in agony on a cross. At best Christianity is seen as a spineless, apathetic, listless, half-hearted approach to life. It may enable its followers to *survive* in this world (this 'vale of tears' as they call it!), but certainly not to *flourish* or find gratification and delight in the experience of living.

Swinburne and Nietzsche

In Victorian times this attitude was well conveyed by Algernon Charles Swinburne (1837–1909) in a long poem with an appropriately long title: 'Hymn to Proserpine: After the Proclamation in Rome of the Christian Faith'.[2] In powerful lines midway through this poem Swinburne addresses Jesus in these accusatory words: 'Thou hast conquered, O pale Galilean! The world has grown grey from thy breath'. The adjectives, so well chosen, tell it all: 'pale' and 'grey'. And Christianity, following in the footsteps of its founder, has continued to drain the life out of human existence and leave it in a pathetic, dreary, vapid condition.

This example from literature can be paralleled in philosophy by reference to the writings of Swinburne's contemporary, Friedrich Nietzsche (1844–1900). His earliest work, *The Birth of Tragedy*, appeared in 1872. Fourteen years later he appended to it a short piece which he entitled 'A Critical Backward Glance'.

> From the very first, Christianity spelled life loathing itself, and that loathing was simply disguised, tricked out, with notions of an 'other' and 'better' life. A hatred of the 'world', a curse on the affective urges, a fear of beauty and sensuality, a transcendence rigged up to slander mortal existence, a yearning for extinction, cessation of all effort until the great 'Sabbath of Sabbaths' – this whole cluster of distortions, together with the intransigent Christian assertion that nothing counts except moral values, had always struck me as being the most dangerous, most sinister form the will to destruction can take; at all events, as a sign of profound sickness, moroseness, exhaustion, biological etiolation.[3]

Throughout his writings Nietzsche relentlessly condemned what he regarded as the slave-morality of Christians; a morality that is not that of free individuals but is born out of the resentment of weaklings.

Christian Collusion

It cannot be denied that Christians have sometimes, maybe even often, lent substance to this image and these accusations. Puritanism – represented more specifically by Manicheanism in the time of Augustine, by the Albigensian heresy in the Middle Ages, and later by English Puritanism and French Jansenism (in the Reformed and Catholic traditions respectively) – is a phenomenon that keeps resurfacing. Furthermore, over the centuries the teaching of many moral theologians, even among the Fathers of the Church, has been fear-fuelled, rigid and repressive in the area of sexuality. Catechesis and preaching have often given the Christian life a dour, po-faced, killjoy image. And have religious always lived their celibate chastity in a zestful, life-affirming manner? Or have they, through their (distorted) witness, contributed to the negative stereotype of Christian attitudes to sex?

There is also the problem of art. Since the nineteenth century self-styled religious art, sometimes known as repository art, has emasculated the figure of Jesus and desexualised that of Mary. In a parallel development, but over a much longer time-span, the popular perception of saints has been woefully distorted. Uncritical biographies (now more accurately known as hagiographies) have presented the saint as a grotesque caricature of the fully mature human being.

In summary, these wide-ranging reflections may help to situate religious life in a broad anthropological, historical, and cultural context. Chastity, whether marital or celibate, is a virtue unique to sexual beings, and is always lived in and through human relationships – with family, community, friends and colleagues. But the world of relationships is also a world of ambiguities, of uncertainties, of opacity and, ultimately, of mystery. With this in mind we recalled the gods and goddesses of our pagan past to intimate that they are still alive and influencing us. They do so, as we have seen, not only through the surrounding culture where they are rampant, but, as archetypes, through the personal unconscious of each individual.

The gods and goddesses are most obviously the source of our carnal cravings, our lusts, but they also, perhaps more insidiously, sow in us the seeds of a melancholic nostalgia and a corrosive envy. They colonise and sexualise our imaginations. They remind all Christians of what they have lost through modelling themselves on the 'pale Galilean'. They ridicule in particular those pathetic women and men who have recklessly squandered their lives through an obsession with vowed chastity. All the while they themselves remain hidden, invisible, only becoming identifiable through dreams and other manifestations of the unconscious.

Relationship: A Key Christian Value

It is time now to change focus and to turn to human relationships as viewed within the Christian tradition. One of the disadvantages in using the word celibacy (rather than chastity) for the 'second vow' is that its literal meaning is negative: the refusal of marriage, or the state of being unmarried. But if, as religious believe, consecrated chastity is a gift from God, it cannot be something negative and ultimately barren. It is true that this gift can have, indeed does have, side-effects that are experienced as negative. But the gift itself can only be positive. Religious chastity is for living, for loving, for flourishing. It has everything to do with full-blooded interpersonal relationships: with the God of Abraham, Isaac and Jacob; with Jesus, the enfleshed and full revelation of that God; with men and women, near and far, saints and sinners. It implies that religious are called to a life of caring and being cared for, of commitment to people and having people committed to them. It has to do with love received and love given, however imperfectly. Mutuality is all!

Another way of expressing this, now almost a cliché, is that God wants every person to become as fully human and as fully alive as possible. This notion of 'becoming' fits well with contemporary thought. We have moved from an older, static model of the human person to one that is dynamic and fluid. Through the influence of philosophies such as personalism and existentialism on the one hand, and the insights of modern depth and experimental psychologies on the other, the human person is now viewed largely in terms of change, growth, process, freedom and, especially, in terms of relationships. John Henry Newman had anticipated this movement when he wrote: 'In a higher world it is otherwise, but here below to live is to change, and to be perfect is to have changed often.'[4] For the phrase 'to be perfect' we can justifiably read 'to be fully human'. This desire of God that we change, that we grow, that we flourish, is no less exigent for religious than for those who marry.

Renouncing and Not Renouncing

It is important to be clear on what religious renounce in undertaking a commitment to celibate chastity. This is twofold. Firstly, they renounce the physical pleasures accompanying sexual intercourse, as well as all other sexual activities and fantasies whose dynamics pave the way to sexual union. Secondly, religious renounce the emotional, psychological and spiritual potential for growth that is uniquely possible through marriage and parenthood. The second renunciation is by far the more hazardous. This is because what *is* not, and *cannot* be renounced, is the responsibility to love, and through loving to reach their full capacity to flourish as human beings. Anyone unable to become a warm, loving, mature, integrated person without the benefit of marriage and parenthood is not called to be a religious. Often the greater danger to fidelity for religious is not the build-up of uncontrollable sexual urges, but the suppression or deflection of the affective faculties. These can become stifled, even calcified, if religious avoid the risk and challenge of meaningful interpersonal relationships.

In more explicitly theological terms, our relationships with God and with people are closely intertwined. Our experience of being loved by God and loving God is somehow dependent on our experience of being loved by people and loving people. St John wrote: 'Those who say, "I love God", and hate their brothers or sisters, are liars; for those who do not love a brother or sister whom they have seen, cannot love God whom they have not seen'. (1 Jn 4:20) We need to give and receive a love that is tangible in order to give and receive a love that is intangible.

> I looked for my soul but my soul I could not see.
> I looked for my God but my God eluded me.
> I looked for a friend and then I found all three.[5]

Living in Community

The promise a person makes to live in celibate chastity is essentially the same whether one is a hermit, a diocesan priest, a monk or nun, an apostolic religious, a member of a secular institute or a lay consecrated virgin. Yet the context in each of these cases is different, and this will modify and define a person's *experience* of chastity. In the case of religious, life is shared more or less closely with other sisters or brothers in various forms of community. The reality of celibacy and the reality of community are thus intertwined. The quality of one affects the quality of the other. In this environment the inner solitude of each person, which is needed for celibacy, enriches the group; while the communal life and vitality of the group nurtures the celibate commitment of each member.

The second part of this statement, regarding the supportive role of community for the individual celibate, is often underlined. Less attention is paid to the first part. This stresses that solitude (and the silence at its core) is an irreplaceable means to a deepening of sisterly and brotherly relationships within community. It is good to listen carefully to these words of Pope Paul VI writing about religious life:

> The search for intimacy with God involves the truly vital need of a silence embracing the whole being, both for those who must find God in the midst of noise and confusion [active religious], and for [enclosed] contemplatives. Faith, hope and a love for God which is open to the gifts of the Spirit, and also a brotherly [or sisterly] love which is open to the mystery of others, carry with them an imperative need for silence.[6]

'A brotherly or sisterly love open to the mystery of others': Is this not an attractive way to describe the living heart of community? But such love does not simply happen. It is built on certain premises, among which is 'an imperative need for silence'.

Turning from a Catholic to a Lutheran perspective, we encounter a reflection by Dietrich Bonhoeffer in his book *Life Together*. In this short work Bonhoeffer pondered on the two years during which he lived a semi-monastic life in the seminary of the Confessing Church that he had established. He had become disillusioned with the mainstream Evangelical Lutheran Church in Germany and what he saw as its capitulation to the Nazi regime and its poisonous ideology. He rejoiced in his positive experience of Christian community at the seminary, without attempting to minimise its difficulties. Then, in the middle of what could be called a celebration of community life, he wrote:

> Alone you stood before God when he called you; alone you had to answer that call; alone you had to struggle and pray; and alone you will die and give an account to God. You cannot escape from yourself for God has singled you out. If you refuse to be alone you are rejecting Christ's call to you, and you have no part in the community of those who are called.[7]

These would be challenging words in any context. They have that quintessentially Protestant emphasis on the Christian standing under the judgment of God. But in the context of Bonhoeffer's enthusiastic ruminations on community, they are also unexpected, even disconcerting. 'If you refuse to be alone … you have no part in the community of those who are called.' Paul VI would later speak in milder terms (see above), but the underlying message of both men is the same. In recent years religious have sometimes turned to the insights of psychologists and the skills of facilitators to improve the quality of their community living. A gentle satirist might wonder aloud if they could not have achieved this goal more effectively by an increased commitment to silence and solitude. It would also have cost less!

Friendship for Religious

Friendship in the lives of religious takes many forms, is experienced in a variety of environments and has many degrees of intensity. Living in community, religious are first summoned to find and nurture friendship there. Ideally, at least, some close relationships within community may be possible, though never guaranteed. Then there are the people whom religious serve through their ministries and those others who are their co-workers. Friendships of depth may well emerge from these settings. Finally, there are the friendships religious just 'happen' to form, beginning from chance meetings or strange coincidences. These relationships may stretch back over many years. Taken together, all of these offer religious the possibility of enjoying a wide range of relationships such as is healthy and enlivening for any human being, celibate or not. It is an enriching experience to have friends of both sexes among many age groups, different social backgrounds, varied occupations and so on. Through them all religious touch and are touched by life. They also touch and are touched by God.

Moving across the spectrum from nodding acquaintance, to casual friendship, to closer friendship, to deep loving, the authenticity of a person's commitment to chastity becomes more and more pertinent. In simple acquaintance, this commitment is almost inconsequential, but in a relationship of deep loving it moves to centre stage. Some religious are more comfortable occupying a space somewhere around the centre of that spectrum. They feel that their religious chastity is less under threat there. But for others, the call to risk loving another human being at a deep level is part of God's invitation to respond to *God's* love. When such an opportunity arises they accept it with joy, even if this is accompanied by a degree of trepidation. They do not cease to be aware that their chastity is a fragile as well as a beautiful gift, and that it must always be safeguarded as well as honoured.

Such religious also realise that any deep, loving relationship cannot be disconnected from other dimensions of their religious life. If the love is healthy, honest, mutual, life-giving and Spirit-led, the friendship will not simply be religiously neutral. It will be an important contributing factor to the person's integral human and spiritual development. Perhaps paradoxically, it will enhance the depth of the person's prayer, the generosity of their contribution to community living, the seriousness of their commitment to mission and their openness to other relationships. As always, the main criterion in evaluating the friendship will be that offered by Jesus in the gospel: 'You will know them by their fruits'. (Mt 7:16)

Friendship and Permanence

Returning to friendship in the widest sense, religious (as well as others) may need to take on board the aphorism: 'The best is the enemy of the good'. For example, it can be counter-productive to insist that all friendships must be permanent. If that is our conviction, we may well miss the beauty and potential of the wide array of friendships that are transitory or short-lived. The urge to make every friendship permanent, or even one specific friendship, is like that of the three disciples on Mount Tabor. They had experienced a short period of real intimacy with Jesus and, filled with joy, they wanted it to last for ever. But they had to move on, to follow Jesus even as he came down from the mountain and resumed his itinerant ministry. (Mt 17:1–8) Mary Magdalen's desire to cling to the Risen Christ also illustrates this point. (Jn 20:11–18) In fact, all the disciples had to let him go at the Ascension.

It is obvious that these parallels are not exact. For instance, the Risen Lord remained present to his friends through his Spirit. The relationship endured despite its apparent ending. But what I want to emphasise is the *longing* for permanence that these stories exemplify. This longing is innate in us. However, the reality is that some friendships (inside and outside religious life) endure while others do not. This should neither surprise nor dismay us. It is part of the human condition. To accept this reality leads us to keep a light grasp on all our friendships. Enjoy but do not cling! Do not foster false expectations! And above all, religious need to recognise that no friend can be a substitute spouse!

CHAPTER 6

The Obedience That Is Faith[1]

Obedience as All-pervasive

Our whole relationship with God can be experienced and understood
in terms of obedience and disobedience. Obedience is not just one
virtue among other virtues. It is not part of a relationship that is experienced, or that can be explored, in isolation from other parts. Obedience is a component in every virtue. Or, to speak in metaphor, obedience is the soil in which the other virtues take root and grow. Why do
we try to live justly? Because God wills it. Why do we serve the needy?
Because that is what God desires of us. There is an all-pervasiveness
about obedience that has it reaching into every nook and cranny of
our Christian living.

Religious have sometimes been tempted to corner obedience as a
virtue to which only they have been called. Nothing could be further from the truth. The whole of creation is under the authority of
God. The search for the will of God is a responsibility for all people,
even those who have not come to the knowledge of God in Christ.
Submission to God is the central requirement of Islam. Jews look to
the Torah and their Covenant to hear what God's word requires of

them. Humanists and atheists acknowledge the binding authority of conscience, even though their explanation of its presence does not require the existence of a personal God.

Obedience as Listening

The root meaning of the Greek and Latin words that we translate as obedience is *to listen*, or, more accurately, *to listen attentively*. We are called to listen to God as he speaks, communicates and reveals himself in Scripture, in the teaching of the Church, in other people, in the signs of the times, in our consciences and in the stirrings of our hearts. Such listening can take countless forms, from basic self-acceptance, through a willing pursuit of each one's unique calling within the Christian community, to our final *Amen* to the time and manner of our death. In the words of Mary, 'Here I am, the servant of the Lord; let it be with me according to your word'. (Lk 1:38)

It may be surprising to speak of self-acceptance as obedience. Let me explain. Since God is my Creator, the person I am is the person God wants me to be. Of course, this is not to be understood in a static way. Growth and change form an intrinsic part of who we are. It is in God's plan that we be constantly in the process of becoming. Hence we are called, at any 'now' in our lives, to embrace two realities: firstly, our current stage of growth (who we are today), and secondly, the process of future change (who we will become tomorrow). God wills both. Our compliance with this constantly unfolding narrative is obedience.

The vivid dialogue, imagined by Isaiah as taking place between the potter and the clay, illustrates the obedience required of us. It also alerts us to the resistances to self-acceptance that we can experience within ourselves. Envy can be one of them.

Woe to you who strive with your Maker,
Earthen vessels with the potter!

71

> Does the clay say to the one who fashions it,
> 'What are you making?' or 'Your work has no handles'?
> Woe to anyone who says to a father, 'What are you begetting?'
> Or to a woman, 'With what are you in labour?'
> Thus says the Lord, the Holy One of Israel, and its Maker:
> Will you question me about my children,
> Or command me concerning the work of my hands?
> (Is 45:9–11)

Envy reveals much about our level of self-acceptance and our obedience to the God who created us as he wanted each of us to be. Whenever we feel envious of another person's talents, intellect, beauty or personality, it is helpful to return to this passage in Isaiah. But it needs to be entered into prayerfully, with a lively imagination and an openness to be disturbed, disoriented and purified.

After self-acceptance, though overlapping with it to some degree, we are called to listen to what is closest to us: *our embodied selves*. We learn to pay attention to our physical *body* as it reveals its reality and its needs to us, insisting that we respond to it with reverence and concern. We learn to attend to our *soul*, a term encompassing our feelings and emotions, with their fluctuating attractions and aversions. We learn to tune in to our *spirit* as it craves for ultimate meaning, for aesthetic experience and for eventual immortality. Because our embodied selves are such a complex and ever-evolving reality, listening will always be challenging and unremitting. Our presupposition is not that God *sometimes* communicates with us at these different levels, but that he is *always* speaking through our experience of body, soul and spirit. What we need is the sensitivity to pick up his messages and the grace to grow in an obediential attitude.

Next, moving outwards from our personal self-awareness, we are faced with the requirement of listening to others. Who are these others? They are women and men in *their* embodied selves, in their social relationships with us, and as citizens of whatever political society we share. All are mediators of God and of God's plan for us. We might express this in an aphorism: *As the other speaks, so does God communicate.* This statement is not to be taken simplistically, as though the words of the 'other' were literally the words of God. We always need to interpret what God is saying through the mediation of the 'other'. The Ignatian tradition refers to this process of interpretation as discernment. Acting on what we have discerned is obedience.

In a new and urgent way today, listening to the 'other' must include listening to planet Earth and, indeed, the Universe. The meaning of the 'other' has expanded to incorporate the non-human. This stretches the language we use around communication and it becomes even more analogical. But it is the stretching of our imaginations, the expanding of our horizons and the reordering of our priorities that provide us with the greatest challenges. Earlier, when reflecting on poverty, I touched on some of the imperatives that arise when we listen to, and hear, the 'cry of the earth'. We also saw how closely this is connected with the 'cry of the poor'. We might further deepen our understanding of what is at stake by reading *Laudato Si*, not only through the lens of poverty and justice, but also through that of obedience to God, the Creator of all that is.

Obedience as Faith

In both the Old and New Testaments the terms faith and obedience are practically synonyms. Abraham exemplifies this faith-obedience both in his initial response to God's call (Gen 12:1–4) and in his later willingness to sacrifice his son, Isaac. (Gen 22:1–18) In the latter story Abraham is asked by God to offer as a burnt offering 'your son, your only child Isaac, whom you love'. If Abraham had carried this out, it would certainly have been a personal and family calamity. But Isaac was not just Abraham's only child according to the flesh. He was the one person through whom Yahweh had promised to fulfil his promises to the whole people of Israel. His death, therefore, would also have been a religious and national calamity. Both of these consequences caught the attention of the author of the Letter to the Hebrews:

> By faith Abraham, when put to the test, offered up Isaac. He who had received the promises was ready to offer up his only son, of whom he had been told, 'It is through Isaac that descendants shall be named for you'. He considered the fact that God is able even to raise someone from the dead – and figuratively speaking, he did receive him back. (Heb 11:17–19)

The story of the sacrifice of Isaac existed long before the Bible came to be written. In its original form, as part of an oral tradition, its purpose was to teach that Yahweh, unlike the gods of the surrounding nations, did not demand human sacrifice. Even today it is quite possible to read the story in this way and to admire how well the point is made. But the same story, as told in Genesis, has a different purpose. The biblical author's interpretation is conveyed in verse 18, where the Lord says to Abraham: 'And by your offspring shall all the nations of the earth gain blessing for themselves, because you have obeyed my voice.' This new promise extends beyond the people of Israel and now embraces all humankind. What has made this possible? 'Because you [Abraham] have obeyed my voice.' Other translations read 'because you have been obedient to me', or more loosely, 'as a reward for your obedience'. The whole ancient story has been reworked in order to illustrate the centrality in God's eyes of the virtue we call faith-obedience.[2]

Pauline Usage

Paul is in line with this older Jewish tradition when he speaks of 'the obedience of faith'. The genitive case here is what is called apposi-

tional, showing that the phrase, 'the obedience of faith', is equivalent
to 'the obedience that is faith'. As in Genesis the two words are synonyms, or almost synonyms. Paul uses this expression in his Letter to
the Romans, opening with the words:

> Paul, a servant of Jesus Christ, called to be an apostle,
> set apart for the gospel of God ... the gospel concerning
> his Son ... through whom we have received grace and
> apostleship to bring about *the obedience of faith* among all
> the Gentiles for the sake of his name, including your-
> selves who are called to belong to Jesus Christ. (Rom
> 1:1–6)

And he concludes the letter as follows:

> Now to God who is able to strengthen you according
> to my gospel and the proclamation of Jesus Christ, ac-
> cording to the revelation of the mystery that was kept
> secret for long ages but is now disclosed, and through
> the prophetic writings is made known to all the Gentiles,
> according to the command of the eternal God, to bring
> about *the obedience of faith* – to the only wise God, through
> Jesus Christ, to whom be the glory forever! Amen. (Rom
> 16:25–27)

So the phrase 'the obedience of faith' appears in the first and last
sentence of what is arguably Paul's greatest letter. It seems to have had
special significance for his understanding of humankind's relationship
with God. For Paul obedience is not simply a moral virtue, but that
total human response to the Good News that is proclaimed through
the apostolic preaching. It is a surrender in faith to God.

The Obedience of Jesus

The primary model of Christian obedience is that of Jesus to his Father. In the Infancy Narratives we learn a little about the obedience

of the child Jesus to his parents. (Lk 2:51) This does indeed serve as a model for Christian obedience – but only that of a child. Regarding the obedience of the adult Jesus we need to focus on what the gospels tell us of his public life. In reading the evangelists' narrative, we come to realise that the imaginative world of Jesus was saturated by the Father, who was omnipresent to him. He was conscious of coming from the Father and returning to the Father. At his baptism he had heard a voice from heaven saying, 'This is my Son, the Beloved, with whom I am well pleased'. (Mt 3:17) This affirmation was repeated at the Transfiguration. Time and again, particularly in the gospel of John, we see the total fascination that the Father exercised on his human sensibility. His personal sense of identity, the meaning he found in his life, as well as the choices that he made, all came from this profound filial relationship with the Father. Indeed, as he said, 'I and the Father are one'. (Jn 10:30)

The mission of Jesus, therefore, does not come to him from outside himself, but is an intrinsic component of who he is. His identity and his mission are one. He is Son only in so far as he is sent; he is sent only in so far as he is Son. Jesus cannot but be on mission because that is who he is. But paradoxically, since he is human as well as divine, he is free to refuse his mission. This freedom is precisely what the devil homed in on, and tried to manipulate, during the temptations in the desert. (Mt 4:1–11) He attempted to wean Jesus away from the mission he had received from his Father, or at least to distort that mission. However, for Jesus to succumb to this temptation would be to deny his very identity, to be like the pot that rebelled against the potter, wanting to be somebody that he was not. He would deserve the rebuke: 'Woe to anyone who says to a father, "What are you begetting?" '. (Is 45:10) But Jesus remained obedient to his Father, accepting both his identity and his mission.

Jesus speaks of his relationship with his Father a number of times in the gospel of John. In each case he is affirming his obedience. The cumulative effect of these sayings can be compelling.

☞ My food is to do the will of him who sent me, and to complete his work. (4:34)

☞ I can do nothing on my own. As I hear, I judge; and my judgement is just, because I seek to do not my own will but the will of him who sent me. (5:30)

☞ I have come down from heaven, not to do my own will, but the will of him who sent me. (6:38)

☞ I judge no one. Yet even if I judge, my judgement is valid; for it is not I alone who judge, but I and the Father who sent me. (8:15-16)

☞ When you have lifted up the Son of Man, then you will realise that I am he, and that I do nothing on my own, but I speak these things as the Father instructed me. (8:28)

☞ And the one who sent me is with me; he has not left me alone, for I always do what is pleasing to him. (8:29)

As with Jesus, so with us. The more profoundly we appreciate our relationship with the Father as beloved sons and daughters, the more spontaneously an obediential attitude will well up from within us. And, as with Jesus, this will be an expression of our identity, of who we truly are, and of who we yearn to become.

The Obedience of Mary

In reflecting on poverty we saw Mary as one of the *anawim*, a woman who lived in poverty of spirit. There are similarities between poverty of spirit and what we have just described (in Pauline terms) as 'the obedience of faith' or 'the obedience that is faith'. Mary displays this attitude of faith-obedience at the Annunciation, when she listens to what the angel has to say, acknowledges the message as coming from God, explores its meaning and then freely accepts her mission and its consequences. Her obediential attitude is summed up in the words: 'Here am I, the servant of the Lord; let it be with me according to your word'. (Lk 1:38) As with Abraham, Mary's acceptance of God's will, her obedience, is not merely personally sanctifying. Her 'Yes' and its consequences certainly transform her own life, but they also transform the destiny of her race and of Planet Earth. Her obedience has universal implications in the drama that is salvation history.

Mary's role during the public life of Jesus is little commented on in the gospels. This absence of evidence leaves us with tantalising questions concerning her relationship with her adult son as he pursued his mission. Was she present with him more frequently than is recorded? How did she view his activities and his teaching? Did she understand what he was attempting to achieve? Or, like some other family members, did she question his sanity?

> Then he went home; and the crowd came together again, so that they could not even eat. When his family heard it, they went out to restrain him, for people were saying, 'He has gone out of his mind'. (Mk 3:19–21)

However, as well as wondering how Mary regarded her son, we may also ask how her son regarded her. There is the familiar story, recorded in all three synoptics, that allows us to see Mary from Jesus' own perspective:

> Then his mother and his brothers came; and standing outside, they sent to him and called him. A crowd was sitting around him; and they said to him, 'Your mother and your brothers and sisters are outside, asking for you'. And he replied, 'Who are my mother and my brothers?' And looking at those who sat around him, he said, 'Here are my mother and my brothers! Whoever does the will of God is my brother and sister and mother'. (Mk 3:31–35)

Here Jesus is not trying to play down Mary's relationship with him as his mother, or to deny his continuing love for her. However, her arrival, along with his brothers and sisters, offers him an opportunity to speak, not about family but about discipleship. The core of this teaching is that, even more important than the physical bond between mother and son, is the relationship of faith-obedience between any individual person and God. This is not the only occasion where Jesus relativizes, but does not deny, the value of family. But when he praises those who do the will of God, and calls them his 'brother and sister and mother', he is putting faith-obedience at the beating heart of the kingdom. He is also describing the essence of discipleship. As Jesus looks about his audience, at those 'sitting around him', he is addressing them directly. Nevertheless, indirectly he is recognising that Mary, who is 'standing outside', also practises faith-obedience. Mary's obediential attitude makes her too a disciple.

Ecclesial Obedience

Something, however rudimentary, must be said about obedience to (or within) the Church. This will help to build a bridge between the scriptural explorations in this chapter and the reflections on religious obedience in the next. Some readers will be familiar with the 'Rules for Thinking, Judging, and Feeling with the Church' in the Spiritual Exercises (352–70).[3] Given the long period of time that Ignatius spent composing, revising and editing this work, we cannot dismiss these Rules as of minor importance. Ignatius included them because of their contribution to the dynamic of the Exercises. More widely they draw our attention to the centrality of the Church in Ignatian spirituality. The Rules are, of course, time-conditioned, and markedly influenced by the turmoil caused by the Reformation. They need to be reinterpreted in light of the ecclesiology of Vatican II. But to reinterpret does not mean to abandon. Instead, we are challenged to identify their core message, which is as valuable now as it was in the days of Ignatius.[4]

Let us look at the reality of the Church through the lens of mission. The Father sent (missioned) the Son to save or redeem humanity. The Father and the Son together sent (missioned) the Spirit to sanctify or make humanity holy. Through baptism, all who are initiated into 'the community that is Church', are by that very act inserted into this two-pronged saving and sanctifying mission. All the baptised are not only saved and sanctified themselves, but are sent out (missioned) to play a part in the saving and sanctifying of others.

However, the initial recipient of this two-pronged mission is not the individual Christian but the Church. It is only by being brought into communion with the Church that individual believers receive their mission. This mission (first of Church, then of the individual Christian) has its ultimate source in the Father. For the word 'source' we can substitute 'author', from which comes the word 'authority'. The Father, the author, who holds this authority, bequeaths it first to the Son. Then the Risen Christ, through the working of his Spirit, shares this (already mediated) authority with the Church. Without authority, and the means to exercise it, the Church could neither maintain itself in unity nor fulfil its mission.

There is a parallel, although not a complete correspondence, between the authority that exists in the Church and that which exists in a religious institute. In both cases:

- ☞ The ultimate source of authority is God.
- ☞ That authority is mediated (exercised through human beings).
- ☞ An obediential response is required.

It will be helpful to keep these insights in mind as we continue with our musings on the place and value of obedience in religious life.

CHAPTER 7

Obedience Within
Religious Life[1]

Benedict and Nadal

We began our reflections on obedience by tracing the word's roots to the verb 'to listen' or 'to listen intently'. As we move into an explicit consideration of religious obedience, we can see how this etymology influenced the Prologue to the Rule of St Benedict. The opening lines of this influential text read:

Listen, child of God, to the guidance of your teacher. Attend to the message you hear and make sure that it pierces to your heart, so that you may accept with willing freedom, and fulfil by the way you live, the directions that come from your loving Father. It is not easy to accept and persevere in obedience, but it is the way to return to Christ, when you have strayed through the laxity and carelessness of disobedience. My words are addressed to you especially, whoever you may be, whatever your circumstances, who turn from the pursuit of your own self will and ask to enlist under Christ, who is

81

Lord of all, by following him through taking to yourself
that strong and blessed armour of obedience which he
made his own on coming into our world.[2]

These words, at once firm and inspiring, are capable of being appreciated by any religious, contemplative or active. Their appearance at the beginning of the Rule suggests that for Benedict all the values of monastic life can be subsumed under the rubric of obedience. They also point to the obedience of Jesus as the model to follow -- an indubitable teaching, appropriate for Christians in all walks of life. Of course, when we get beyond the fundamental obediential attitude (necessary for all), differences of interpretation and practice begin to arise. Diverse traditions of religious life each have their own charism, which determines, to a great extent, the kind of obedience that is required for authenticity. Such differences have to be recognised and honoured, yet (as with the Rule of St Benedict) behind them always lies a common 'catholic' spirituality capable of nourishing all in religious life.

Another rich example may be culled from the Jesuit tradition. Jerome Nadal was a close friend and confidant of Ignatius Loyola, although not one of his first companions. Among his many writings he kept a spiritual journal in which he wrote (addressing himself):

Embrace and diligently exercise that union with Christ
Jesus and his power with which the Spirit of the Lord
has graced you. Then you will know in your spirit that
you are thinking with Christ's thoughts, willing with
Christ's will, and remembering with Christ's memory.
You will know that you exist, and are living and acting
not just as yourself, but completely in Christ.[3]

Jerome goes on to describe such an awareness as the highest perfection in this life, as a divine strength in the person graced in this way, and as a marvellous sweetness or consolation. He does not mention the word obedience, but what he writes here offers a profound vision of what that virtue entails: 'thinking with Christ's thoughts, willing with Christ's will, and remembering with Christ's memory ... living and acting not just as yourself but completely in Christ'. If obedience does not lead to and express such union with Christ, if it is not at heart a contemplative or mystical experience, then a vital component is missing.

A Corporate Starting Point

Discussions of obedience usually begin by focusing on the individual religious. However, I am choosing to take a corporate starting point. Some religious refer to the institute (order or congregation) to which they belong as a family. For a number of reasons Ignatius Loyola pre-ferred to regard the Society of Jesus as a body. He used this term in a way that is analogous to that of Paul describing the Church as the body of Christ.

> Indeed, the body does not consist of one member but of many. If the foot would say, 'Because I am not a hand, I do not belong to the body', that would not make it any less a part of the body. And if the ear would say, 'Because I am not an eye, I do not belong to the body', that would not make it any less a part of the body. If the whole body were an eye, where would the hearing be? If the whole body were hearing, where would the sense of smell be? But as it is, God arranged the members in the body, each one of them, as he chose. If all were a single member, where would the body be? As it is, there are many members, yet one body. (1 Cor 12:14–20)

While recognising that 'body' is not the only helpful metaphor for a religious institute, I will continue to employ it in these reflections. There need not be anything exclusively Jesuit about such usage.

Religious obedience begins with the commitment of the entire institute, the body, to seek the will of God. This is because God, through the institute's founder(s), has first called the body into being and animated it up to this moment in history. It is the body as a whole that is gifted with the fullness of the charism. It is also this body that is sent, that is entrusted with its particular mission, and that must respond by implementing that mission. Consequently, it is the body that is first called to obey. At any particular time the corporate attitude of the institute may be more or less faithful, more or less obediential, more or less open to the Spirit, and so more or less Christ-like.

What then of the individual religious? Where do they fit into this narrative? Firstly, the individual members, each in their own time and circumstances, share in the charism and the mission of the body in so far as they are fully and lovingly integrated into its corporate life. Secondly, the individual members may be more or less in harmony with the attitude of the body taken as a whole (its corporate attitude). These ideas may need to be teased out further.

There are four possible scenarios. The most positive and healthy is when the institute or body and an individual member are in full harmony in seeking and responding to the will of God. The most negative and unhealthy is when the institute or body and an individual member are equally deaf and resistant to what God is asking. Both body and individual are following their own agenda out of a loss of faith, or because of laziness, disillusionment, cynicism or lack of freedom. This may look like harmony of a sort, but it is an empty, meaningless charade.

However, two other scenarios are also possible. The institute, the body, may be sensitively alert to the signs of God's will, while an individual member may be negligently or even contumaciously resistant and deaf. On the other hand, the body as a whole may have become complacent or lethargic, while an individual member may be listening to God with eagerness and docility. Such a person may become a lonely, prophetic voice in the wilderness calling the body to obedience. Often this plea will either be ignored or ridiculed. The bearer of the message, the prophet, will be regarded as a dreamer or a troublemaker. These third and fourth scenarios give rise to obvious tensions which often erupt in conflict. Obedience and disobedience cannot peacefully coexist.

A Sense of Belonging

It is worth exploring further the situation where the body, the institute, is truly listening to God and is open to whatever God wants. As a result, it has begun a corporate discernment process, aimed at discovering the best way forward, and at setting appropriate, yet challenging, apostolic goals. What sort of issues now face the individual religious living under obedience? Consider the case of Sarah.[4] What will her attitude be? How will she respond? If Sarah has an unwavering sense of belonging within the body, if she has put down deep roots over the years, she will willingly, actively and enthusiastically participate in the corporate search for God's will. She will also feel committed to the implementation of whatever decisions emerge. Conversely, if Sarah's sense of belonging is fragile or tentative or unsure, even more if she feels alienated from the body, she will be inclined to opt out of the discernment process and be unconcerned about its outcome.

Disaffection or apathy of this kind is objectively a failure in obedience. Whether such failure is culpable, or to what degree, is another matter. That will depend on many subjective factors. It is easy to imagine Sarah rationalising her negative attitude by adopting a narrowly legalistic approach to authority. She may continue doing whatever she is told (at least within certain limits), practising what tradition has called the obedience of execution. She may see herself as a hard worker, committed to 'her' ministry. But Sarah will obstinately refuse to take any part in, or accept any responsibility for, the institute's corporate search for God's will. She might say, 'Tell me what to do and I'll do it, but don't ask me to go to meetings!' At best this attitude reveals an individualistic or privatised spirituality that is incompatible with contemporary religious life.

Wellspring and Confirmation of Union

By beginning with a focus on the corporate, we can readily see how obedience is a source or wellspring of union within the body. Simultaneously, obedience gives practical expression to that union and attests to its authenticity. It can be said to confirm that union. The corporate search for the will of God, in accordance with the charism of the institute, is what chiefly bonds the members of any apostolic body. Engagement in this search forges the union of minds and hearts.

Such discernment will be practised in an intense and concentrated way whenever major decisions are necessitated. However, discernment is not something that can be switched on and off as needed. It has to be a familiar atmosphere in which the members feel comfortable, indeed it has to be a way of life. It begins with the practice of personal discernment but goes beyond it. If a community as such is not discerning in its day-to-day living – prayerfully attending to the signs of God's will – the members will not suddenly become discerning persons when crises arise. Structures, such as *révision de vie*, may be needed, so that each member's personal discernment, nurtured in their own prayer, may contribute to a corporate experience through open and amicable sharing.

Obedience as Christ Centred

From the beginnings of religious life the person of Christ has always been central in the theology and practice of obedience. This Christocentric understanding has led religious to value obedience as an inter-personal encounter with their Lord. Indeed, as we saw in the case of Jerome Nadal, such obedience can become a profoundly contemplative or mystical experience. Its foundation will be a steady, contemplative gaze that enables a person to recognise Christ in that place of interaction between authority and obedience. Given such a contemplative gaze (or stance), a religious grows into an increasingly intimate union with Christ in two ways.

Firstly, the religious recognises in the authority of the superior[5] the mediated authority of Christ, and (a further step) recognises in the person of the superior the person of Christ. Both of these 'recognitions' or acknowledgements come from a faith vision without which obedience would not be religious.[6]

Secondly, the religious enters into, or takes on, the obediential attitude of Christ. The Risen Lord does not offer our obedience to the Father as something extrinsic to himself. Rather, since we died and rose with him in baptism, our obedience becomes part of his obedience, a prolongation of it in today's world. This is similar to the way that our prayer becomes part of Christ's prayer, and reaches the Father as the prayer of the Whole Christ. It becomes the prayer of the Body of Christ, head and members. So too our obedience and that of Christ are one.

Drawing together these two aspects of religious obedience, we can say that it is both *obedience to Christ* present in the superior, and a sharing in the *obedience of Christ* as he responds with filial love to his and our Father.

Obedience and Asceticism

Some element of asceticism, self-discipline and struggle always exists in the practice of obedience. There are both positive and negative reasons for this. Positively, one of the marks of the mature person is autonomy. The journey from childhood to adulthood is in large part a growth in our desire for, capacity for, and exercise of autonomy. But since we live in a human community, we learn from an early age that this autonomy has to be balanced by the demands of interpersonal, social and political realities. Accepting the need for such balance, and integrating the consequent limitations of our autonomy, are also part of the maturation process. All of this already presumes an ongoing asceticism.

Negatively, there are the realities of sin and disorder. The basically healthy drive towards autonomy is vitiated by an unhealthy drive towards egoism and pride. While human autonomy can never be total, and we can concede this readily enough in theory, yet we are constantly beguiled by Satan's promise, 'You will be like gods'. (Gen 3:5) It is significant that the sin of Adam (humankind) is presented in Scripture as disobedience arising from an overweening desire for autonomy – indeed the autonomy of God himself.

Against this background the ascetical aspect of obedience becomes clearer. Obedience is a human virtue, an attitudinal habit that can only be learned through its exercise. We do not become obedient by reading about it or discussing it. Asceticism, however, is not an end in itself. It is a means towards what we really want. From an ascetical perspective, the aim and outcome of exercising ourselves in obedience is growth into a genuine inner freedom. This will prevent our being manipulated either by outside influences, such as those of the prevailing culture, or by the disorder within our own selves. The resulting inner freedom will then express itself in availability for mission.

Obedience as Mission Oriented

In so far as obedience is a union with the obediential will of Christ, it is also a union with the salvific will of the Father, 'who desires everyone to be saved and to come to the knowledge of the truth'. (1 Tim 2:4) The obediential attitude of religious has them wanting whatever

Christ and the Father want. In this general sense obedience is always at the service of the redemptive work of Christ. However, in explicitly apostolic institutes the link between obedience and this redemptive work is more precise and direct. Here obedience is *primarily* related to mission, and might even be called an 'instrument' of mission. Through the mutuality that is involved in the interface between authority and obedience, mission, which originates with the Father, is mediated to the institute and then to the individual members. The primary expression of such obedience is the acceptance of the institute's mission and then one's own. All other expressions of obedience are secondary.

More on Discernment

Many religious have become relatively comfortable in discerning on a personal level. But from time to time religious are also called to engage in a process of discernment that is specifically communal. They face a decision that is not going to be made by each individual separately (even if in a community context), but a decision emanating from and implicating the community itself – be that local, regional or worldwide. Communal discernment is not just the sum total of the personal discernment processes of each community member. The subject of communal discernment is the corporate entity: the body, the WE. What do we discern to be the will of God for US? Therefore, each person in the group must first be conscious of the bond that holds the members together, that makes them a body rather than a loose association of individuals. Each and all must be aware of, and must own, their common vocation, purpose, charism and mission.

To get in touch with this reality it can be helpful to practise what is sometimes dubbed corporate *anamnesis*. Religious, as a body, recall their history, and in so doing bring to awareness their corporate experience of God. It will be a history of light and dark, of consolation and desolation, of grace and sin. This recollection will throw light on their corporate identity and strengthen their sense of union and of purpose. All this needs to be firmly in place at a time when many attitudinal differences, many diverse aspirations and dreams, are likely to surface. The cohesion of the body may be severely tested. So too may the inner freedom of each person, as well as the inner freedom of the group. However, when there is a union of hearts and minds, rooted in a shared memory, the body will emerge unscathed and enhanced. Then the obedience that accepts the final decision will bring peace and joy.

Toxic or Life-giving?

It is commonly assumed that the three traditional religious vows are counter-cultural. On the whole this is true. However, the values that religious try to live through their vows are not always in conflict with those of secular society. For example, respect for the vow of poverty has increased in recent years. A simpler, more sustainable lifestyle is being put forward, not only as an acceptable societal option, but even as a moral imperative. Such an ideal of living more simply, usually based on environmental concerns, may not have the radicalism of a commitment to be poor with the poor Christ. Nevertheless, it builds a bridge between the secular and religious mind-sets.

It may be more difficult to imagine such a bridge in relation to chastity. Yet even here, some of the values that religious proclaim through the vow of chastity surface in secular discussions around the side-effects of the sexual revolution, the abuse of women and children in the home, pornography and so forth. Some secular feminist writers have even tried to claim celibacy (non-marriage) as a feminist value.[7]

Obedience, however, is taboo. There is no strand of contemporary western culture that will defend it, still less propose it as something positive. Increasingly around the world, freedom is the highest value.

Freedom of nations, free elections, freedom of thought, freedom of the press, religious freedom, academic freedom, freedom of choice and so on – the list is endless. Even those who want to move away from an exaggerated individualism are not interested in restoring obedience as a social value. It is seen as the antithesis of freedom. (Of course, from their faith perspective religious see obedience as leading to a greater freedom – but this makes no sense in the secular world).

There are impelling historical reasons for this distrust and rejection of obedience. The worst excesses of the fascist regimes in Europe in the 1930s and 1940s could not have occurred outside of an accepted culture of blind obedience. Even people of sophisticated intelligence and apparently high integrity left their religious and human values aside when ordered to do so. 'I was acting under orders' was the only defence that these military or civilian personnel could make when faced with their crimes. Obedience to orders had become the only moral or ethical value in these totalitarian regimes.

Closer to home, the Church has had to endure the scandal of physical and sexual abuse of children and young adults by religious and clergy. Some of this occurred in institutional settings such as orphanages and industrial schools, but it also occurred in wider pastoral settings. Throughout this moral débâcle the role played by a distorted understanding of authority and obedience is difficult to assess, but that it did play a role is certain. The religious and clergy who perpetrated the abuse were all living under authority and professed to be obedient. But those who held this authority failed in their duty of care, in large part because they did not really know their members. The openness and transparency that should exist between those holding authority and those living under it were either absent or had become a pretence. On both sides there was culpable irresponsibility. Any obedience that was practised was extrinsic, impersonal and possibly manipulative.

This malformation inevitably affected the individual religious when they found themselves in authority over children and young adults. They demanded obedience – but obedience of an external, indeed of a servile kind. This was done, and then justified, as a means to maintain discipline in stressful circumstances. But strict discipline frequently evolved into physical abuse, and sometimes into sexual abuse. We have come to recognise that sexual abuse is more an expression of the will to control than an acting-out of the sexual drive itself. Hence the physical and sexual abuse were not totally different from each other. In both instances the submission, the obedience of the children and young adults, was degrading and dehumanising.

All of this past and recent history has made the vow of obedience problematic in new ways. Can it be rehabilitated? Or should it be quietly set aside and forgotten, as it seems to have been by a small minority of religious (in practice if not in theory)? If obedience is understood in extrinsic, authoritarian, or even purely ascetical terms, it probably should be left to die. However, the best of the Christian tradition approaches obedience with a radically different attitude, so much so that it is unrecognisable when set beside the distortions I have been considering. Obedience, as I have emphasised, is above all a contemplative exercise, founded on an experiential relationship with God. It is Christ-centred and in service of his mission. It is energised by 'God's love … poured into our hearts through the Holy Spirit'. (Rom 5:5) Such obedience enriches the spiritual life of an institute and its members, increases rather than diminishes their inner freedom, and witnesses to the sovereignty of God in human life.

CODA

When Pauline was a little girl her family used to bring her on holidays
to a lovely location in a remote part of the country. Among many
attractions on offer Pauline's favourite was a majestic waterfall which
she never tired of visiting. Nearby was a summer house in which there
were different-coloured windows. Three of these looked out directly
onto the waterfall. One was red, another yellow and the third blue.
Pauline used to skip around from one window to another in wonder
and delight, as the waterfall changed from red to yellow to blue It
was sheer bliss! At first she even thought that there might be three
waterfalls. But Pauline was a bright girl and she gradually came to
realise that there were not three waterfalls but one! No matter what
the colour the waterfall was always the same waterfall.

Many years later, when Pauline had become a religious, she used to
recall this childhood experience when talking about the three vows.
The waterfall of her childhood represented the total commitment
that she had made to God; the different coloured windows stood
for the vows. Poverty, chastity and obedience were lenses through
which she contemplated her one commitment, and which lit it
up (as it where) in assorted hues. But the vows were never really
separate from each other, and they certainly did not create three
unconnected commitments! Rather (to change the metaphor) her
poverty, chastity and obedience flowed into each other as did the

mountain streams that fed the waterfall.

Pauline's appreciation of the oneness of her commitment is shared by most religious as they grow older. In the early years of religious life it will be necessary to focus on each of the vows individually in order to understand, appreciate and integrate them into one's life. But once that is achieved the process of 'unification' begins. Without always realising it these mature religious are then on the same wavelength as the Fathers and Mothers of the Desert. They, as we saw in Chapter 1, thought and spoke of the one 'renunciation', their complete letting-go into the hands of God. Such was and remains the goal of religious life.

NOTES

Prologue
1. *Acta Apostolicae Sedis*, vol. CVI, no. 12 (5 December 2014), 935–47

Chapter 1: The Origins of Religious Life
1. The word 'liminality' comes from the Latin for threshold. It refers to the experience of being in an in-between space or state, of living in two worlds, of being related to the divine and earthly. This engenders a heightened sensibility, new ways of knowing, all leading to a more profound wisdom.
2. 'Desert' in this context is often better translated as a wilderness or a harsh, barren landscape. It does not always imply a desert of sand.
3. Shortly after Antony's death a ground-breaking biography appeared: Athanasius (Bishop of Alexandria), *The Life of Antony and the Letter to Marcellinus*, trans. R. Gregg. New York: Paulist Press (1980).
4. *The Spiritual Exercises of Saint Ignatius*, trans. G. Ganss. Chicago: Loyola University Press (1992).
5. *Early Christian Writings: The Apostolic Fathers*, trans. M. Staniforth/A. Louth. Harmondsworth: Penguin Classics (1987), 86.
6. Ibid. 87
7. Rowan Williams, *The Wound of Knowledge*. London: DLT (1979), 19–20. The author rewrote this passage in the book's second, revised edition (1990), 21.
8. Op. cit.

Chapter 2: The Biblical Roots of Poverty
1. Augustine of Hippo, *The Monastic Rules*, trans. Sr Agatha Mary and G. Bonner. New York: New City Press (2004), 110.
2. The remainder of this chapter, and all of the next (Chapter 3), are a reworking of an earlier article: B. O'Leary, 'Poverty Revisited', *Religious Life Review*, vol. 54 (May–June 2015), 151–63.
3. The Revised English Bible has a lively translation of the last verse: 'Then what is my pay? It is the satisfaction of preaching the gospel without expense to anyone; in other words, of waiving the rights my preaching gives me.'
4. John Cassian, *The Institutes*, trans. B. Ramsay OP (*Ancient Christian Writers*, n. 58) New York, NY/Mahwah, NJ (2000), 79–80.
5. Ibid. 98.

Chapter 3: Religious Poverty: A Synthesis of Values

1. Also known as the *Regula non bullata* (1221).
2. *Francis and Clare: The Complete Works*, trans. R. Armstrong and I. Brady. New York, NY/Ramsey, NJ/Toronto: Paulist Press (1982), 109.
3. Ibid. 116.
4. See earlier comments on these texts in Chapter 1.
5. *Didache*, trans. J. Kleist (*Ancient Christian Writers*, n. 6). Cork: Mercier Press (1948), 17.
6. Pope Francis, *Laudato Sí*, n. 222. Dublin: Veritas (2015), 112.
7. 'Come to me, all you that are weary and are carrying heavy burdens, and I will give you rest' (Mt 11: 28).
8. *Saint Benedict's Rule*, trans. P. Barry. Mahwah, NJ: Hidden Spring (1997), 123–24.
9. Simone Weil, *Waiting on God*, trans. E. Craufurd. Glasgow: Collins (1951/1978), 17.
10. 'Those who are oppressed by poverty are the object of *a preferential love* on the part of the Church', *Catechism of the Catholic Church*, n. 2448. Dublin: Veritas (1994), 523.
11. Pope Francis, *Evangelii Gaudium*, n. 198. Dublin: Veritas (2013), 103.
12. Pope Francis, *Laudato Sí*, n. 48. Dublin: Veritas (2015), 29.
13. *Francis and Clare*, op. cit., 197.
14. *The Spiritual Exercises of Saint Ignatius*, op. cit., 73
15. *The Constitutions of the Society of Jesus and their Complementary Norms*, n. 101, trans. J. Padberg. St Louis, MO: Institute of Jesuit Sources (1996), 46.

Chapter 4: Biblical Wisdom Behind Chastity

1. In the remainder of this chapter I have drawn extensively on John Lozano, *Discipleship: Towards an Understanding of Religious Life*, trans. B. Wilczynski. Chicago: Claret Center for Resources in Spiritualty (1980), 144–58.
2. For a fuller discussion of the rabbinic tradition, see Harvey McArthur, 'Celibacy in Judaism at the Time of Christian Beginnings', in *Andrews University Seminary Studies*, vol. 25, no. 2 (summer 1987), 163–81.
3. A. Flannery (General Editor), *Vatican II. The Basic Sixteen Documents: Constitutions, Decrees, Declarations*. Dublin: Dominican Publications (1996), 68.
4. I am simplifying this argument for the sake of brevity and clarity. The English translations are not as distinct in meaning as I am making them.

5. E. Schillebeeckx, *Clerical Celibacy Under Fire*, London: Sheed & Ward (1968), 15.

Chapter 5: Chastity and Human Maturity

1. Jean Shinoda Bolen, *Goddesses in Everywoman: A New Psychology of Women* (1985); *Gods in Everyman: A New Psychology of Men's Lives and Loves* (1989). New York: Harper & Row.
2. *The Poems of Algernon John Swinburne*, vol. 1. *Poems and Ballads: First Series*. London: Chatto & Windus (1905, 67–73.
3. Friedrich Nietzsche, *The Birth of Tragedy and the Genealogy of Morals*, trans. F. Golffing. New York: Doubleday Anchor Books (1956), 10–11.
4. J. H. Newman, *An Essay on the Development of Christian Doctrine*, 1, 1, 7. New York: Doubleday Image Books (1960), 63.
5. Anon. (although sometimes attributed to William Blake).
6. Pope Paul VI, *Evangelica Testificatio*, n. 46. London: Catholic Truth Society (1975), 46.
7. Dietrich Bonhoeffer, *Life Together*, trans. J. W. Doberstein. London: SCM Press (1954), 57.

Chapter 6: The Obedience That Is Faith

1. This is a reworking of an earlier article: B. O'Leary, 'Christian and Religious Obedience', in D. Fleming (ed.), *Paths of Renewal for Religious*. St Louis, MO: Review for Religious (1986), 195–201.
2. 'The great Old Testament archetype of obedience (and, therefore, of faith) is Abraham, whose trust in God brings him to the point where he is ready to give back to the Lord that which is most precious to him – his future. God asks for Isaac, the long-awaited rightful heir, and in a way that is impossible for the old man to understand at the time, his obedience paradoxically returns to him what he is prepared, at great personal cost, to give back to God.' R. Maas, *New Dictionary of Catholic Spirituality*, ed. M. Downey. s.v. 'obedience', Collegeville, MN: The Liturgical Press (1993), 709.
3. *The Spiritual Exercises of Saint Ignatius*, op. cit., 133–37.
4. Highly recommended is a recent book that pursues these objectives: Gill K. Goulding CJ, *A Church of Passion and Hope. The Formation of an Ecclesial Disposition from Ignatius Loyola to Pope Francis and the New Evangelization*. London: Bloomsbury (2015).

Chapter 7: Obedience Within Religious Life

1. This is a reworking of an earlier article: B. O'Leary, 'Wellspring of Union: Reflections on Obedience', *Religious Life Review*, vol. 47 (July–

August 2008), 247–56.

2. *Saint Benedict's Rule*, trans. P. Barry, Mahwah, NJ: Hidden Spring (1997), 45.

3. Jerome Nadal, *Orationis Observationes*, ed. M. Nicolau, in *Monumenta Historica Societatis Iesu*, vol. 90. Rome (1964), 122.

4. A fictional name, meant to indicate a male or female religious.

5. I have chosen this traditional word for the person who holds religious authority. There is nothing sacrosanct about it and some institutes have replaced it with terms such as 'leader'.

6. Such a theological position needs to be presented in a nuanced way; otherwise it can be manipulated by an authority that seeks to dominate.

7. Worth reading is the account by Dawn Eden of her journey from Jewish family roots, first to Protestant and then to Catholic Christianity, and, finally, to a commitment to celibate chastity. Her book is entitled *The Thrill of the Chaste: Fulfilment While Keeping Your Clothes On*. Notre Dame, IN: Ave Maria Press (2015), Catholic edition.

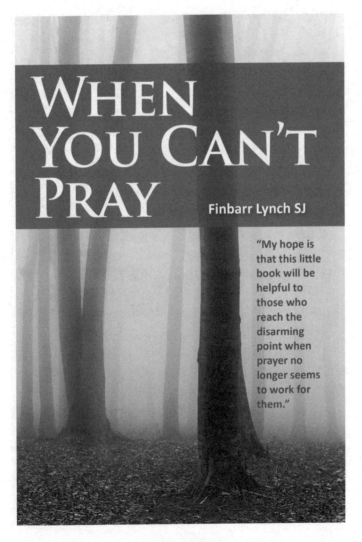

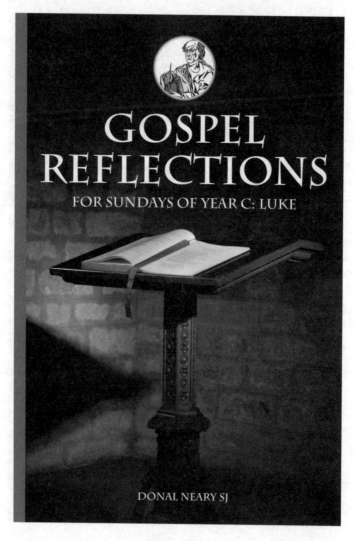

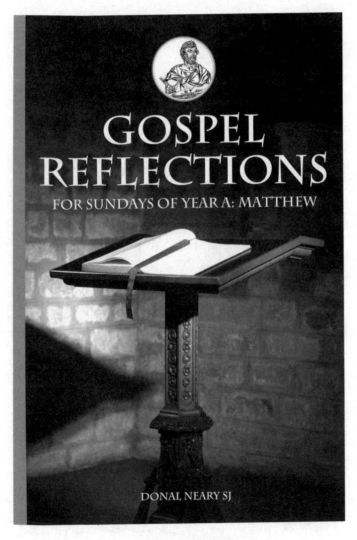

INTO EXTRA TIME

LIVING THROUGH THE FINAL STAGES OF CANCER AND JOTTINGS ALONG THE WAY

MICHAEL PAUL GALLAGHER

€12.99

FORM 6A

Notice Seeking Possession of a Property Let on an Assured Shorthold Tenancy

Housing Act 1988 section 21(1) and (4) as amended by section 194 and paragraph 103 of Schedule 11 to the Local Government and Housing Act 1989 and section 98(2) and (3) of the Housing Act 1996

- Please write clearly in black ink. Please tick boxes where appropriate.
- This form should be used where a no fault possession of accommodation let under an assured shorthold tenancy (AST) is sought under section 21(1) or (4) of the Housing Act 1988.
- There are certain circumstances in which the law says that you cannot seek possession against your tenant using section 21 of the Housing Act 1988, in which case you should not use this form. These are:

  (a) during the first four months of the tenancy (but where the tenancy is a replacement tenancy, the four month period is calculated by reference to the start of the original tenancy and not the start of the replacement tenancy – see section 21(4B) of the Housing Act 1988);

  (b) where the landlord is prevented from retaliatory eviction under section 33 of the Deregulation Act 2015;

  (c) where the landlord has not provided the tenant with an energy performance certificate, gas safety certificate or the Department of Communities and Local Government's publication "How to rent: the checklist for renting in England" (see the Assured Shorthold Tenancy Notices and Prescribed Requirements (England) Regulations 2015);

  (d) where the landlord has not complied with the tenancy deposit protection legislation; or

  (e) where a property requires a licence but is unlicensed.

  Landlords who are unsure about whether they are affected by these provisions should seek specialist advice.

- This form must be used for all ASTs created on or after 1 October 2015 except for statutory periodic tenancies which have come into being on or after 1 October 2015 at the end of fixed term ASTs created before 1 October 2015. There is no obligation to use this form in relation to ASTs created prior to 1 October 2015, however it may nevertheless be used for all ASTs.

WHAT TO DO IF THIS NOTICE IS SERVED ON YOU

- You should read this notice very carefully. It explains that your landlord has started the process to regain possession of the property referred to in section 2 below.
- You are entitled to at least two months' notice before being required to give up possession of the property. However, if your tenancy started on a periodic basis without any initial fixed term a longer notice period may be required depending on how often you are required to pay the rent (for example, if you pay rent quarterly, you must be given at least three months' notice, or, if you have a periodic tenancy which is half yearly or annual, you must be given at least six months' notice (which is the maximum)). The date you are required to leave should be shown in section 2 below. After this date the landlord can apply to court for a possession order against you.
- Where your tenancy is terminated before the end of a period of your tenancy (e.g. where you pay rent in advance on the first of each month and you are required to give up possession in the middle of the month), you may be entitled to repayment of rent from the landlord under section 21C of the Housing Act 1988.
- If you need advice about this notice, and what you should do about it, take it immediately to a citizens' advice bureau, a housing advice centre, a law centre or a solicitor.

G000017230

Continued overleaf

1. **TO:**

   Name(s) of tenant(s) (Block Capitals) _____

   _____

   _____

2. You are required to leave the below address after _____ .[1]

   If you do not leave, your landlord may apply to the court for an order under section 21(1) or (4) of the Housing Act 1988 requiring you to give up possession.

   Address of premises _____

   _____

   _____

3. This notice is valid for six months only from the date of issue unless you have a periodic tenancy under which more than two months' notice is required (see notes accompanying this form) in which case this notice is valid for four months only from the date specified in section 2 above.

4. **Name and address of landlord**

   To be signed and dated by the landlord or their agent (someone acting for them). If there are joint landlords each landlord or the agent must sign unless one signs on behalf of the rest with their agreement.

   SIGNED _____ **DATE** _____

   Please specify whether: Landlord ☐   Joint landlords ☐   Landlord's agent ☐

   Name(s) of signatory/signatories (Block Capitals) _____

   _____

   _____

   _____

   Address(es) of signatory/signatories _____

   _____

   _____

   _____

   _____

   Telephone of signatory/signatories _____

   _____

[1] Landlords should insert a calendar date here. The date should allow sufficient time to ensure that the notice is properly served on the tenant(s). This will depend on the method of service being used and landlords should check whether the tenancy agreement makes specific provision about service. Where landlords are seeking an order for possession on a periodic tenancy under section 21(4) of the Housing Act 1988, the notice period should also not be shorter than the period of the tenancy (up to a maximum of six months), e.g. where there is a quarterly periodic tenancy, the date should be three months from the date of service.

Contains public sector information licensed under the Open Government Licence v3.0.

HOUSING ACT 1988
SECTION 21
Assured Shorthold Tenancy : Notice Requiring Possession

WALES

TO _____

of _____

_____

FROM _____

of _____

_____

I/We* give you notice that, by virtue of Section 21 of the Housing Act 1988, I/we* require possession (*delete as appropriate)
of the dwelling house known as

_____

after _____

or, if the alternative date mentioned below is different, after the alternative date. The alternative date is the first date after this notice was given to you which is:

- at least two months after service upon you of this notice, and

- (if your tenancy is for a fixed term which has not ended when this notice is given to you) which is a date not earlier than the end of the fixed term, or

- (if your tenancy is a periodic tenancy when this notice is given to you) which is the last day of a period of your tenancy and not earlier than the earliest date on which your tenancy could (apart from the landlord's inability, under s.5(1) of the Housing Act 1988, to terminate an assured tenancy by notice to quit) lawfully be ended by a notice to quit given to you on the same date as this notice.

DATED _____

SIGNED _____Landlord/Landlord's agent* (*delete as appropriate)

_____

_____

_____

Tenant's acknowledgment of service

I/We acknowledge the service of the notice of which the above is a true copy.

Signed_____ (Tenant(s))   Date_____

Note: This notice may be validly served even if this box has not been signed by the tenant

---

HOUSING ACT 1988 SECTION 8

As amended by section 151 of the Housing Act 1996 and section 97 of the Anti-social Behaviour, Crime and Policing Act 2014

NOTICE SEEKING POSSESSION OF A PROPERTY LET ON AN ASSURED TENANCY OR AN ASSURED AGRICULTURAL OCCUPANCY

- Please write clearly in black ink.
- Please cross out text marked with an asterisk (*) that does not apply.
- This form should be used where possession of accommodation let under an assured tenancy, an assured agricultural occupancy, or an assured shorthold tenancy is sought on one of the grounds in Schedule 2 to the Housing Act 1988.

- Do not use this form if possession is sought on the 'shorthold' ground under section 21 of the Housing Act 1988 from an assured shorthold tenant where the fixed term has come to an end or, for assured shorthold tenancies with no fixed term which started on or after 28th February 1997, after six months has lapsed. There is no prescribed form for these cases, but you must give notice in writing.

---

1 To _____

     Name of tenant(s)

---

2 Your landlord intends to apply to the court for an order requiring you to give up possession of: _____

     _____

     _____

     _____

     Address of premises

---

3 Your landlord intends to seek possession on grounds 8, 10 and 11 in Schedule 2 to the Housing Act 1988, as amended by the Housing Act 1996, which read:

Ground 8

Both at the date of the service of the notice under section 8 of this Act relating to the proceedings for possession and at the date of the hearing -

a) if rent is payable weekly or fortnightly, at least eight weeks' rent is unpaid;
b) if rent is payable monthly, at least two months' rent is unpaid;
c) if rent is payable quarterly, at least one quarter's rent is more than three months in arrears; and
d) if rent is payable yearly, at least three months' rent is more than three months in arrears.

and for the purpose of this ground "rent" means rent lawfully due from the tenant.

Ground 10

Some rent lawfully due from the tenant -

a) is unpaid on the date on which the proceedings for possession are begun; and
b) except where subsection (1)(b) of section 8 of this Act applies, was in arrears at the date of the service of the notice under that section relating to those proceedings.

Ground 11

Whether or not any rent is in arrears on the date on which proceedings for possession are begun, the tenant has persistently delayed paying rent which has become lawfully due.

---

4 Particulars of each ground are as follows:

Grounds 8, 10 and 11

The tenant is currently in arrears of rent of £ _____ .
[A schedule showing how the arrears are calculated is annexed to this notice.]*

_____

_____

_____

_____

_____

Give a full explanation of why each ground is being relied on. Continue on a separate sheet if necessary.

*If there is a complex arrears history, a schedule is advised; otherwise delete.

Notes on the grounds for possession

- If the court is satisfied that any of grounds 1 to 8 is established, it must make an order (but see below in respect of fixed term tenancies).
- Before the court will grant an order on any of grounds 9 to 17, it must be satisfied that it is reasonable to require you to leave. This means that, if one of these grounds is set out in section 3, you will be able to suggest to the court that it is not reasonable that you should have to leave, even if you accept that the ground applies.
- The court will not make an order under grounds 1, 3 to 7, 9 or 16, to take effect during the fixed term of the tenancy (if there is one), and it will only make an order during the fixed term on grounds 2, 8, 10 to 15 or 17 if the terms of the tenancy make provision for it to be brought to an end on any of these grounds.
- Where the court makes an order for possession solely on grounds 6 or 9, the landlord must pay your reasonable removal expenses.

---

5 The court proceedings will not begin until after:

_____

(Give the earliest date on which court proceedings can be brought)

Notes on the earliest date on which court proceedings can be brought

- Where the landlord is seeking possession on grounds 1, 2, 5 to 7, 9 or 16 (without ground 7A or 14), court proceedings cannot begin earlier than 2 months from the date this notice is served on you and not before the date on which the tenancy (had it not been assured) could have been brought to an end by a notice to quit served at the same time as this notice. This applies even if one of grounds 3, 4, 8, 10 to 13, 14ZA, 14A, 15 or 17 is specified.
- Where the landlord is seeking possession on grounds 3, 4, 8, 10 to 13, 14ZA, 14A, 15 or 17 (without ground 7A or 14), court proceedings cannot begin earlier than 2 weeks from the date this notice is served. If one of 1, 2, 5 to 7, 9 or 16 grounds is also specified court proceedings cannot begin earlier than two months from the date this notice is served.
- Where the landlord is seeking possession on ground 7A (with or without other grounds), court proceedings cannot begin earlier than 1 month from the date this notice is served on you and not before the date on which the tenancy (had it not been assured) could have been brought to an end by a notice to quit served at the same time as this notice. A notice seeking repossession on ground 7A must be served on you within specified time periods which vary depending on which condition is relied upon:
  - Where the landlord proposes to rely on condition 1, 3 or 5: within 12 months of the conviction (or if the conviction is appealed: within 12 months of the conclusion of the appeal);
  - Where the landlord proposes to rely on condition 2: within 12 months of the court's finding that the injunction has been breached (or if the finding is appealed: within 12 months of the conclusion of the appeal);
  - Where the landlord proposes to rely on condition 4: within 3 months of the closure order (or if the order is appealed: within 3 months of the conclusion of the appeal).
- Where the landlord is seeking possession on ground 14 (with or without other grounds other than ground 7A), court proceedings cannot begin before the date this notice is served.
- Where the landlord is seeking possession on ground 14A, court proceedings cannot begin unless the landlord has served, or has taken all reasonable steps to serve, a copy of this notice on the partner who has left the property.
- After the date shown in section 5, court proceedings may be begun at once but not later than 12 months from the date on which this notice is served. After this time the notice will lapse and a new notice must be served before possession can be sought.

---

6 Name and address of landlord:

To be signed and dated by the landlord or his agent (someone acting for him). If there are joint landlords each landlord or the agent must sign unless one signs on behalf of the rest with their agreement.

Signed _____   Dated _____

_____

Please specify whether: Landlord ☐   Joint Landlord ☐   Landlord's Agent ☐

Name(s) (Block capitals) _____

_____

_____

Address: _____

_____

_____

_____

Telephone Daytime _____   Evening _____

What to do if this notice is served on you

- This notice is the first step requiring you to give up possession of your home. You should read it very carefully.
- Your landlord cannot make you leave your home without an order for possession issued by a court. By issuing this notice, your landlord is informing you that he intends to seek such an order. If you are willing to give up possession without a court order, you should tell the person who signed this notice as soon as possible and say when you are prepared to leave.
- Whichever grounds are set out in section 3 of this form, the court may allow any of the other grounds to be added at a later date. If this is done, you will be told about it so you can discuss the additional grounds at the court hearing as well as the grounds set out in section 3.
- If you need help or advice about this notice and what you should do about it, take it immediately to a citizens' advice bureau, a housing advice centre, a law centre, or a solicitor.

SHORT ASSURED TENANCY NOTICE TO QUIT

SCOTLAND

NOTICE OF REMOVAL UNDER SECTION 37 OF THE
SHERIFF COURTS (SCOTLAND) ACT 1907

FROM:
LANDLORDS

(name and address)

_____

_____

_____

TO:
TENANT

(name and address)

_____

_____

_____

DATE: _____

PROPERTY: _____

_____

The above Landlords hereby give notice to the above Tenant that the Tenant is required to remove from the above property at the _____day of _____ in terms of Lease between the Landlords and the Tenant dated _____.

(insert dates)

The undernoted schedule which is incorporated herein complies with the Assured Tenancies (Notice to Quit Prescribed Information) (Scotland) Regulations 1988.

SIGNED

_____
(Landlord(s), or Landlord(s)'s Agent with full name and address)

SCHEDULE

1. Even after the Notice to Quit has run out, before the tenant can be lawfully evicted, the landlord must get an Order for Possession from the Court.

2. If the Landlord issues a Notice to Quit but does not seek to gain possession of the Property in question the contractual assured tenancy which has been terminated will be replaced by a Statutory Assured Tenancy. In such circumstances the Landlord may propose new terms for the tenancy and may seek an adjustment in rent at annual intervals thereafter.

3. If a tenant does not know what kind of tenancy he has or is otherwise unsure of his rights he can obtain advice from a Solicitor. Help with all or part of the cost of legal advice and assistance can be available under the Legal Aid Legislation. A tenant can also seek help from a Citizens Advice Bureau or Housing Advisory Centre.

SECTION 33 LANDLORD'S NOTICE TO TERMINATE

SHORT ASSURED TENANCY

SCOTLAND

FROM:
LANDLORDS _____ *(name and address)*

_____

_____

TO:
TENANT _____ *(name and address)*

_____

_____

DATE: _____

PROPERTY: _____

_____

The above Landlords hereby give formal notice to the above Tenant under Section 33 of the Housing (Scotland) Act 1988 of their intention to bring the Tenant's tenancy to an end and recover possession of the above property currently occupied by the Tenant.

In terms of Section 33 of the aforementioned Act the Tenant must receive at least two months notice of the Landlords' intention to recover possession. Please therefore take note that you require to vacate the premises no later than _____ *(insert dates)*

SIGNED _____

(Landlord(s), or Landlord(s)'s Agent with full name and address)

NOTE
This Notice to Terminate and a Notice to Quit should both be completed and sent to the Tenant at least two months before the end of the tenancy.

Part 4   Proceedings will not be raised before _____ which is the earliest date at which proceedings can be raised under Section 19 of the Housing (Scotland) Act 1988).

SIGNED   _____

(Landlord(s) or Landlord(s)'s Agent)

DATED   _____

Note 4 to Tenant. If your Landlord does not raise court proceedings this notice AT6 will cease to have effect 6 months after the earliest date on which court proceedings could have been raised (See Part 4 of the Notice).

Note 5 to Tenant. If you want to consent your Landlord's intention to repossess your home, you are strongly advised to take legal advice without delay and before the expiry of the time limit given by the notice. Help with all or part of the cost of legal advice may be available under the legal aid legislation.

Note 6 to Prospective Tenant. Remember before you must leave your home, your Landlord must have done 3 things:
1. Served on you a Notice to Quit (Note carefully that this may have been served at an earlier stage in the tenancy to change the tenancy from a Contractual to a Statutory Assured Tenancy); and
2. Served on you an AT6 (this Notice): and
3. Obtained a court order.

Note 7 to Tenant. This is an important document and you should keep it in a safe place.

The Assured Tenancies (Forms) (Scotland) Regulations 1988 are reproduced under the terms of the Open Government Licence

ASSURED TENANCIES
HOUSING (SCOTLAND) ACT 1988

AS AMENDED BY PARAGRAPH 85 OF SCHEDULE 17
TO THE HOUSING ACT 1988
NOTICE UNDER SECTION 19 OF INTENTION TO RAISE PROCEEDINGS FOR POSSESSION

IMPORTANT: INFORMATION FOR PROSPECTIVE TENANT(S)
This notice informs you as tenant that your landlord intends to apply to the Sheriff for an Order for possession of the house at the address in Part 1, which is currently occupied by you.

PLEASE READ THIS NOTICE CAREFULLY

Part 1   To _____

         of _____

           _____

           _____

Note 1 to Tenant. If you are uncertain about what this notice means, or if you are in doubt about anything in it, or about its validity or whether it is filled in properly you should immediately consult a solicitor or an organisation which gives advice on housing matters. You may also find it helpful to discuss this notice with your landlord.

(name of tenant(s)

(address of house)

Part 2   I/We (on behalf of)* your landlord(s)

    _____

    of _____

        _____

(name(s) of landlord(s))

(address and telephone number o~~r~~ landlord(s)

inform you that I intend to raise proceedings for possession of the house at the address in Part 1 above on the following grounds being grounds for possession as set out in Schedule 5 to the Housing (Scotland) Act 1988.

*Ground 8 - Both at the date of the service of this notice and at the date of the hearing at least three months' rent lawfully due by tenant is in arrears and more specific arrears of rent are £_____.

*Ground 12 - Some rent lawfully due by tenant is in arrears at the date of service of this notice namely, £_____ due on _____ 20_____.

Note 2 to the Tenant. A full list of the 17 Grounds for Possession in Schedule 5 to the Housing (Scotland) 1988 together with information on your rights as Tenant is given in the booklet ' Assured Tenancies in Scotland. A Guide for Landlords and Tenants'. It is available from any office of the Rent Assessment Committee, Citizens Advice Bureau, Housing Advisory Centre or from the Rent Registration Service.

(give the ground number (s) and fully state grounds(s) as s~~e~~ out in Schedule 5 to the Housing (Scotlan~~d~~ Act 1988: continue o~~n~~ additional sheets of paper if required)

*delete as appropria~~te~~

Part 3   I/we* also inform you that I/we are seeking possession under the above ground/grounds* for the following reasons:-

    _____

    _____

    _____

(state particulars of how you believe the ground(s) have arise~~n~~ continue on addition~~al~~ sheets of paper if required)

Note 3 to Tenant. Your Landlord must give you proper notice between serving this Notice and raising court proceedings. If any of Grounds 1,2,5,6,7,9 and 17 apply with or without other Grounds, 2 months notice must be given. Your Landlord must also give you 2 months notice if your tenancy is a Short Assured Tenancy and your Landlord is seeking repossession on the ground that the Tenancy Period has expired. If only other grounds apply, only 2 weeks notice need be given.

NOTES FOR LANDLORDS TO BE READ WITH NOTICE AT5.
THESE NOTES ARE FOR GUIDANCE ONLY AND ARE NOT A DEFINITIVE INTERPRETATION OF THE LAW

WHEN TO USE THIS NOTICE

1. You should use this notice only when you wish to inform a prospective tenant or tenants that the tenancy being offered by you is a short assured tenancy under Section 32 of the Housing (Scotland) Act 1988.

2. You must serve the notice on the prospective tenant or tenants before the creation of any tenancy agreement. If it is not served before the creation of the tenancy agreement the tenancy will not be a short assured tenancy.

ABOUT SHORT ASSURED TENANCIES

3. A short assured tenancy is a special form of assured tenancy which in the first instance must be for not less than 6 months. It gives you special rights to repossess the house (see paragraph 4) and special rights for tenants to apply to a Rent Assessment Committee for a rent determination (see paragraphs 5 and 6).

   Repossession of the Property

4. As landlord, if you obtain a possession order from the Sheriff, you may repossess the house you are letting on the short assured tenancy. Before applying for a possession order you must

   4.1 Issue a valid notice to quit to terminate the tenancy at its expiry date, and not offer your tenant another tenancy;

   4.2 Give your tenant notice of your intention to apply for the order. The notice must be for at least 2 months unless your tenancy agreement provides for a longer period. If you fulfil these two conditions the Sheriff must grant you the order.

5. Unless a rent for the tenancy has already been determined by a Rent Assessment Committee, a tenant of a short assured tenancy has a right to seek a rent determination from a Rent Assessment Committee at any time during the tenancy. On receiving an application, the Committee will consider if it is appropriate to determine a market rent.

6. The Rent Assessment Committee will make a rent determination only if it considers there is a sufficient number of similar houses in the locality let on assured tenancies and the rent payable for the tenancy is significantly higher than the landlord might reasonably expect to charge having regard to rent levels for those tenancies. A rent determination made by the Committee will be the maximum payable for the tenancy from the date specified.

HOW TO USE THIS NOTICE

7. Before you and your prospective tenant make a binding agreement to let a house, you should complete Parts 1, 2 and 3 of the Notice. The Notice should then be given or sent to the prospective tenant or tenants. The tenancy will be a short assured tenancy as long as you have fulfilled all your requirements. The tenant should keep the Notice with the written document setting out the terms of the tenancy which have been agreed, and which must be provided by a landlord under Section 30 of the Housing (Scotland) Act 1988. You are also advised to keep a copy of Notice AT5 for your own records.

FURTHER GUIDANCE

8. If you are uncertain about the question of tenancy status or uncertain about how to complete this Notice, you should consult a solicitor or any organisation which gives advice on housing matters.

9. Further guidance on assured and short tenancies is available in 'Assured Tenancies Scotland - a Guide for Landlords and Tenants'. Copies can be obtained from any office of the Rent Assessment Panel, Citizens Advice Bureau, Housing Advisory Centre or from any office of the Rent Registration Service.

NOTE 4 TO PROSPECTIVE TENANT. A tenant of a short assured tenancy has a special right to apply to a rent assessment committee for a rent determination for the tenancy.

NOTE 5 TO PROSPECTIVE TENANT. If you agree to take up the tenancy after your landlord has served this notice on you your tenancy will be a short assured tenancy. You should keep this notice in a safe place along with the written document setting out the terms of tenancy which your landlord must provide under section 30 of the Housing (Scotland) Act 1988 once the terms are agreed.

NOTE 6 TO PROSPECTIVE TENANT. If you require further guidance on assured and short assured tenancies, consult a solicitor or any organisation which gives advice on housing matters.

SPECIAL NOTES FOR EXISTING TENANTS

1. If you already have a regulated tenancy, other than a short tenancy, should you give it up and take a new tenancy in the same house or another house owned by the same landlord, that tenancy cannot be an assured tenancy or a short assured tenancy. Your tenancy will continue to be a regulated tenancy.

2. If you have a short tenancy under the Tenant's Rights etc. (Scotland) Act 1980 or the Rent (Scotland) Act 1984 your landlord can offer you an assured tenancy or short assured tenancy of the same or another house on the expiry of your existing tenancy.

3. If you are an existing tenant and are uncertain about accepting the proposed short assured tenancy you are strongly advised to consult a solicitor or any organisation which gives advice on housing matters.

The Assured Tenancies (Forms) (Scotland) Regulations 1988 are reproduced under the terms of the Open Government Licence

ASSURED TENANCIES
HOUSING (SCOTLAND) ACT 1988

NOTICE UNDER SECTION 32 TO BE SERVED ON A
PROSPECTIVE TENANT OF A SHORT ASSURED TENANCY

IMPORTANT: INFORMATION FOR PROSPECTIVE TENANT(S)
This notice informs you as prospective tenant(s) that the tenancy being offered by the prospective landlord(s) is a short assured tenancy under Section 32 of the Housing (Scotland) Act 1988.

PLEASE READ THIS NOTICE CAREFULLY

Part 1

_____

_____

(name of prospective tenant(s))

> **Note 1 to prospective tenant.** To be valid this notice must be served before the creation of a tenancy agreement. A short assured tenancy will not exist if a valid notice has not been served.

Part 2

I your prospective landlord(s)/I your prospective landlord's agent*

*(*delete as appropriate)*

of _____ (name of landlord(s))

_____ (address and telephone number of landlord(s))

_____

give notice that the tenancy being offered to you of the house at

_____ (address of house)

_____

to which this notice relates is to be a short assured tenancy in terms of Section 32 of the Housing (Scotland) Act 1988.

> **Note 2 to prospective tenant.** A short assured tenancy is a special form of tenancy. Unless it follows immediately after another short assured tenancy of the same house, (with the same tenant) it must be for not less than 6 months.

SIGNED

_____

(Landlord(s) or Landlord(s)'s Agents)

DATED

_____

Part 3   Address and telephone number of agents if appropriate.

Landlord(s) agent: _____

_____

_____

Tenant(s) agent: _____

_____

_____

> **Note 3 to prospective tenant.** A landlord of a short assured tenancy has special rights to repossess the house. If the landlord terminates the tenancy by issuing a valid notice to quit and gives the tenant at least 2 months' notice (or a longer period if the tenancy agreement provides) of his intention to repossess the house the court must grant the landlord an order allowing him to evict the tenant if he applies for one at the end of the tenancy period set out in the tenancy agreement.

Augmented Reality for Android Application Development

Learn how to develop advanced Augmented Reality applications for Android

Jens Grubert

Dr. Raphael Grasset

BIRMINGHAM - MUMBAI

Augmented Reality for Android Application Development

Copyright © 2013 Packt Publishing

First published: November 2013

Production Reference: 1191113

Published by Packt Publishing Ltd.
Livery Place
35 Livery Street
Birmingham B3 2PB, UK.

ISBN 978-1-78216-855-3

www.packtpub.com

Cover Image by Suresh Mogre (suresh.mogre.99@gmail.com)

Credits

Authors

Jens Grubert

Dr. Raphael Grasset

Reviewers

Peter Backx

Glauco Márdano

Acquisition Editor

Kunal Parikh

Owen Roberts

Commissioning Editor

Poonam Jain

Technical Editors

Monica John

Siddhi Rane

Sonali Vernekar

Copy Editors

Brandt D'Mello

Sarang Chari

Tanvi Gaitonde

Gladson Monteiro

Sayanee Mukherjee

Adithi Shetty

Project Coordinator

Sherin Padayatty

Proofreader

Simran Bhogal

Indexer

Rekha Nair

Production Coordinator

Alwin Roy

Cover Work

Alwin Roy

About the Authors

Jens Grubert is a researcher at the Graz University of Technology. He has received his Bakkalaureus (2008) and Dipl.-Ing. with distinction (2009) at Otto-von-Guericke University Magdeburg, Germany. As a research manager at Fraunhofer Institute for Factory Operation and Automation IFF, Germany, he conducted evaluations of industrial Augmented Reality systems until August 2010. He has been involved in several academic and industrial projects over the past years and is the author of more than 20 international publications. His current research interests include mobile interfaces for situated media and user evaluations for consumer-oriented Augmented Reality interfaces in public spaces. He has over four years of experience in developing mobile Augmented Reality applications. He initiated the development of a natural feature tracking system that is now commercially used for creating Augmented Reality campaigns. Furthermore, he is teaching university courses about Distributed Systems, Computer Graphics, Virtual Reality, and Augmented Reality.

Website: www.jensgrubert.com.

I want to thank my family, specifically Carina Nahrstedt, for supporting me during the creation of this book.

Dr. Raphael Grasset is a senior researcher at the Institute for Computer Graphics and Vision. He was previously a senior researcher at the HIT Lab NZ and completed his Ph.D. in 2004. His main research interests include 3D interaction, computer-human interaction, augmented reality, mixed reality, visualization, and CSCW. His work is highly multidisciplinary; he has been involved in a large number of academic and industrial projects over the last decade. He is the author of more than 50 international publications, was previously a lecturer on Augmented Reality, and has supervised more than 50 students. He has more than 10 years of experience in **Augmented Reality (AR)** for a broad range of platforms (desktop, mobile, and the Web) and programming languages (C++, Python, and Java). He has contributed to the development of AR software libraries (ARToolKit, osgART, and Android AR), AR plugins (Esperient Creator and Google Sketchup), and has been involved in the development of numerous AR applications.

Website: www.raphaelgrasset.net.

About the Reviewers

Peter Backx has an MoS and a PhD. in Computer Sciences from Ghent University. He is a software developer and architect. He uses technology to shape unique user experiences and build rock-solid, scalable software.

Peter works as a freelance consultant at www.peated.be and shares his knowledge and experiments on his blog www.streamhead.com.

Glauco Márdano is a 22-year-old who lives in Brazil and has a degree in Systems Analysis. He has worked for two years as a Java web programmer and he is now studying and getting certified in Java.

He has reviewed the *jMonkeyEngine 3.0 Beginners Guide* book.

I'd like to thank all from the jMonkeyEngine forum because I've learnt a lot of new things since I came across the forum and I'm very grateful for their support and activity. I'd like to thank the guys from Packt Publishing, too, and I'm very pleased to be a reviewer for this book.

www.PacktPub.com

Support files, eBooks, discount offers and more

You might want to visit www.PacktPub.com for support files and downloads related to your book.

Did you know that Packt offers eBook versions of every book published, with PDF and ePub files available? You can upgrade to the eBook version at www.PacktPub.com and as a print book customer, you are entitled to a discount on the eBook copy. Get in touch with us at service@packtpub.com for more details.

At www.PacktPub.com, you can also read a collection of free technical articles, sign up for a range of free newsletters and receive exclusive discounts and offers on Packt books and eBooks.

http://PacktLib.PacktPub.com

Do you need instant solutions to your IT questions? PacktLib is Packt's online digital book library. Here, you can access, read and search across Packt's entire library of books.

Why Subscribe?

- Fully searchable across every book published by Packt
- Copy and paste, print and bookmark content
- On demand and accessible via web browser

Free Access for Packt account holders

If you have an account with Packt at www.PacktPub.com, you can use this to access PacktLib today and view nine entirely free books. Simply use your login credentials for immediate access.

Table of Contents

Preface

Augmented Reality offers the magic effect of blending the physical world with the virtual world and brings applications from your screen into your hands. Augmented Reality redefines advertising and gaming as well as education in an utterly new way; it will become a technology that needs to be mastered by mobile application developers. This book enables you to practically implement sensor-based and computer vision-based Augmented Reality applications on Android. Learn about the theoretical foundations and practical details of implemented Augmented Reality applications. Hands-on examples will enable you to quickly develop and deploy novel Augmented Reality applications on your own.

What this book covers

Chapter 1, Augmented Reality Concepts and Tools, introduces the two major Augmented Reality approaches: sensor-based and computer vision-based Augmented Reality.

Chapter 2, Viewing the World, introduces you to the first basic step in building Augmented Reality applications: capturing and displaying the real world on your device.

Chapter 3, Superimposing the World, helps you use JMonkeyEngine to overlay high-fidelity 3D models over the physical world.

Chapter 4, Locating in the World, provides the basic building blocks to implement your own Augmented Reality browser using sensors and GPS.

Chapter 5, Same as Hollywood – Virtual on Physical Objects, explains you the power of the Vuforia™ SDK for computer vision-based AR.

Chapter 6, Make It Interactive – Create the User Experience, explains how to make Augmented Reality applications interactive. Specifically, you will learn how to develop ray picking, proximity-based interaction, and 3D motion gesture-based interaction.

Chapter 7, Further Reading and Tips, introduces more advanced techniques to improve any AR application's development.

What you need for this book

If you want to develop Augmented Reality applications for Android, you can share a majority of tools with regular Android developers. Specifically, you can leverage the power of the widely supported **Android Developer Tools Bundle (ADT Bundle)**. This includes:

- The Eclipse **Integrated Development Environment (IDE)**
- The **Android Developer Tools (ADT)** plugin for Eclipse
- The Android platform for your targeted devices (further platforms can be downloaded)
- The Android emulator with the latest system image

Besides this standard package common to many Android development environments, you will need:

- A snapshot of **JMonkeyEngine (JME)**, Version 3 or higher
- **Qualcomm® Vuforia™ SDK (Vuforia™)**, version 2.6 or higher
- **Android Native Development Kit (Android NDK)**, version r9 or higher

Who this book is for

If you are a mobile application developer for Android and want to get to the next level of mobile app development using Augmented Reality, then this book is for you. It is assumed that you are familiar with Android development tools and deployment. It is beneficial if you have experience on working with external libraries for Android, as we make use of JMonkeyEngine and the Vuforia™ SDK. If you have already used the Android NDK, then this is great but not mandatory.

Conventions

In this book, you will find a number of styles of text that distinguish between different kinds of information. Here are some examples of these styles and an explanation of their meaning.

Code words in text, database table names, folder names, filenames, file extensions, pathnames, dummy URLs, user input, and Twitter handles are shown as follows: "Finally, you register your implementation of the `Camera.PreviewCallback` interface in the `onSurfaceChanged()` method of the `CameraPreview` class."

A block of code is set as follows:

```
public static Camera getCameraInstance() {
  Camera c = null;
  try {
    c = Camera.open(0);
  } catch (Exception e) { ... }
  return c;
}
```

New terms and **important words** are shown in bold. Words that you see on the screen, in menus or dialog boxes for example, appear in the text like this: " in the pop-up menu, go to **Run As | 1 Android Application**."

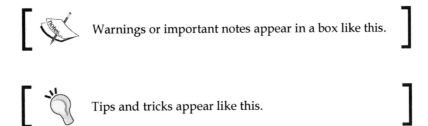

Warnings or important notes appear in a box like this.

Tips and tricks appear like this.

Reader feedback

Feedback from our readers is always welcome. Let us know what you think about this book—what you liked or may have disliked. Reader feedback is important for us to develop titles that you really get the most out of.

To send us general feedback, simply send an e-mail to `feedback@packtpub.com`, and mention the book title via the subject of your message.

If there is a topic that you have expertise in and you are interested in either writing or contributing to a book, see our author guide on `www.packtpub.com/authors`.

Customer support

Now that you are the proud owner of a Packt book, we have a number of things to help you to get the most from your purchase.

Downloading the example code

You can download the example code files for all Packt books you have purchased from your account at http://www.packtpub.com. If you purchased this book elsewhere, you can visit http://www.packtpub.com/support and register to have the files e-mailed directly to you. You can also find the code files at https://github.com/arandroidbook/ar4android.

Errata

Although we have taken every care to ensure the accuracy of our content, mistakes do happen. If you find a mistake in one of our books—maybe a mistake in the text or the code—we would be grateful if you would report this to us. By doing so, you can save other readers from frustration and help us improve subsequent versions of this book. If you find any errata, please report them by visiting http://www.packtpub.com/submit-errata, selecting your book, clicking on the **errata submission form** link, and entering the details of your errata. Once your errata are verified, your submission will be accepted and the errata will be uploaded on our website, or added to any list of existing errata, under the Errata section of that title. Any existing errata can be viewed by selecting your title from http://www.packtpub.com/support.

Piracy

Piracy of copyright material on the Internet is an ongoing problem across all media. At Packt, we take the protection of our copyright and licenses very seriously. If you come across any illegal copies of our works, in any form, on the Internet, please provide us with the location address or website name immediately so that we can pursue a remedy.

Please contact us at copyright@packtpub.com with a link to the suspected pirated material.

We appreciate your help in protecting our authors, and our ability to bring you valuable content.

Questions

You can contact us at questions@packtpub.com if you are having a problem with any aspect of the book, and we will do our best to address it.

Augmented Reality Concepts and Tools

1

Augmented Reality (AR) offers us a new way to interact with the physical (or real) world. It creates a modified version of our reality, enriched with digital (or virtual) information, on the screen of your desktop computer or mobile device. Merging and combining the virtual and the real can leverage a totally new range of user experience, going beyond what common apps are capable of. Can you imagine playing a first-person shooter in your own neighborhood, with monsters popping up at the corner of your street (as it is possible with ARQuake by *Bruce Thomas* at the University of South Australia, see left-hand side of the following screenshot)? Will it not be a thrilling moment to go to a natural history museum and see a dusty dinosaur skeleton coming virtually alive — flesh and bone — in front of your eyes? Or can you imagine reading a story to your kid and seeing some proud rooster appear and walk over the pages of a book (as it is possible with the AR version of the "House that Jack Built" written by *Gavin Bishop*, see the right-hand side of the following screenshot). In this book, we show you how to practically implement such experiences on the Android platform.

A decade ago, experienced researchers would have been among the few who were able to create these types of applications. They were generally limited to demonstration prototypes or in the production of an ad hoc project running for a limited period of time. Now, developing AR experiences has become a reality for a wide range of mobile software developers. Over the last few years, we have been spectators to great progresses in computational power, the miniaturization of sensors, as well as increasingly accessible and featured multimedia libraries. These advances allow developers to produce AR applications more easily than ever before. This already leads to an increasing number of AR applications flourishing on mobile app stores such as Google Play. While an enthusiastic programmer can easily stitch together some basic code snippets to create a facsimile of a basic AR application, they are generally poorly designed, with limited functionalities, and hardly reusable. To be able to create sophisticated AR applications, one has to understand what Augmented Reality truly is.

In this chapter, we will guide you toward a better understanding of AR. We will describe some of the major concepts of AR. We will then move on from these examples to the foundational software components for AR. Finally, we will introduce the development tools that we will use throughout this book, which will support our journey into creating productive and modular AR software architecture.

Ready to change your reality for Augmented Reality? Let's start.

A quick overview of AR concepts

As AR has become increasingly popular in the media over the last few years, unfortunately, several distorted notions of Augmented Reality have evolved. Anything that is somehow related to the real world and involves some computing, such as standing in front of a shop and watching 3D models wear the latest fashions, has become AR. Augmented Reality emerged from research labs a few decades ago and different definitions of AR have been produced. As more and more research fields (for example, computer vision, computer graphics, human-computer interaction, medicine, humanities, and art) have investigated AR as a technology, application, or concept, multiple overlapping definitions now exist for AR. Rather than providing you with an exhaustive list of definitions, we will present some major concepts present in any AR application.

Sensory augmentation

The term Augmented Reality itself contains the notion of reality. Augmenting generally refers to the aspect of influencing one of your human sensory systems, such as vision or hearing, with additional information. This information is generally defined as digital or virtual and will be produced by a computer. The technology currently uses **displays** to overlay and merge the physical information with the digital information. To augment your hearing, modified headphones or earphones equipped with microphones are able to mix sound from your surroundings in real-time with sound generated by your computer. In this book, we will mainly look at visual augmentation.

Displays

The TV screen at home is the ideal device to perceive virtual content, streamed from broadcasts or played from your DVD. Unfortunately, most common TV screens are not able to capture the real world and augment it. An Augmented Reality display needs to simultaneously show the real and virtual worlds.

One of the first display technologies for AR was produced by *Ivan Sutherland* in 1964 (named "The Sword of Damocles"). The system was rigidly mounted on the ceiling and used some CRT screens and a transparent display to be able to create the sensation of visually merging the real and virtual.

Since then, we have seen different trends in AR display, going from static to wearable and handheld displays. One of the major trends is the usage of **optical see-through** (OST) technology. The idea is to still see the real world through a semi-transparent screen and project some virtual content on the screen. The merging of the real and virtual worlds does not happen on the computer screen, but directly on the retina of your eye, as depicted in the following figure:

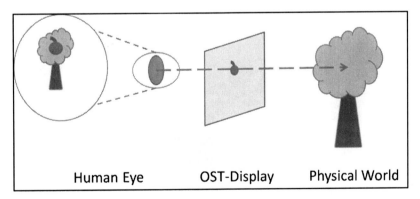

The other major trend in AR display is what we call **video see-through (VST)** technology. You can imagine perceiving the world not directly, but through a video on a monitor. The video image is mixed with some virtual content (as you will see in a movie) and sent back to some standard display, such as your desktop screen, your mobile phone, or the upcoming generation of head-mounted displays as shown in the following figure:

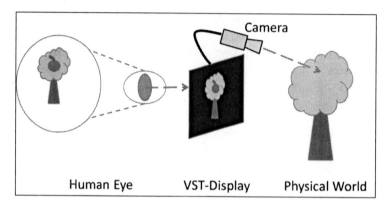

In this book, we will work on Android-driven mobile phones and, therefore, discuss only VST systems; the video camera used will be the one on the back of your phone.

Registration in 3D

With a display (OST or VST) in your hands, you are already able to superimpose things from your real world, as you will see in TV advertisements with text banners at the bottom of the screen. However, any virtual content (such as text or images) will remain fixed in its position on the screen. The superposition being really static, your AR display will act as a **head-up display (HUD)**, but won't really be an AR as shown in the following figure:

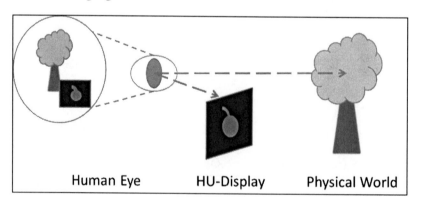

Google Glass is an example of an HUD. While it uses a semitransparent screen like an OST, the digital content remains in a static position.

AR needs to know more about real and virtual content. It needs to know where things are in space (**registration**) and follow where they are moving (**tracking**).

Registration is basically the idea of aligning virtual and real content in the same space. If you are into movies or sports, you will notice that 2D or 3D graphics are superimposed onto scenes of the physical world quite often. In ice hockey, the puck is often highlighted with a colored trail. In movies such as *Walt Disney's* TRON (1982 version), the real and virtual elements are seamlessly blended. However, AR differs from those effects as it is based on all of the following aspects (proposed by *Ronald T. Azuma* in 1997):

- **It's in 3D**: In the olden days, some of the movies were edited manually to merge virtual visual effects with real content. A well-known example is Star Wars, where all the lightsaber effects have been painted by hand by hundreds of artists and, thus, frame by frame. Nowadays, more complex techniques support merging digital 3D content (such as characters or cars) with the video image (and is called match moving). AR is inherently always doing that in a 3D space.

- **The registration happens in real time**: In a movie, everything is pre-recorded and generated in a studio; you just play the media. In AR, everything is in real time, so your application needs to merge, at each instance, reality and virtuality.

- **It's interactive**: In a movie, you only look passively at the scene from where it has been shot. In AR, you can actively move around, forward, and backward and turn your AR display — you will still see an alignment between both worlds.

Interaction with the environment

Building a rich AR application needs interaction between environments; otherwise you end up with pretty, 3D graphics that can turn boring quite fast. AR interaction refers to selecting and manipulating digital and physical objects and navigating in the augmented scene. Rich AR applications allow you to use objects which can be on your table, to move some virtual characters, use your hands to select some floating virtual objects while walking on the street, or speak to a virtual agent appearing on your watch to arrange a meeting later in the day. In *Chapter 6, Make It Interactive – Create the User Experience*, we will discuss mobile-AR interaction. We will look at how some of the standard mobile interaction techniques can also be applied to AR. We will also dig into specific techniques involving the manipulation of the real world.

Choose your style – sensor-based and computer vision-based AR

Previously in this chapter, we discussed what AR is and elaborated on display, registration, and interaction. As some of the notions in this book can also be applied to any AR development, we will specifically look at **mobile AR**.

Mobile AR sometimes refers to any transportable, wearable AR system that can be used indoors and outdoors. In this book, we will look at mobile AR with the most popular connotation used today—using handheld mobile devices, such as smartphones or tablets. With the current generation of smartphones, two major approaches to the AR system can be realized. These systems are characterized by their specific registration techniques and, also, their interaction range. They both enable a different range of applications. The systems, sensor-based AR and computer vision-based AR, are using the video see-through display, relying on the camera and screen of the mobile phone.

Sensor-based AR

The first type of system is called sensor-based AR and generally referred to as a GPS plus inertial AR (or, sometimes, outdoor AR system). Sensor-based AR uses the location sensor from a mobile as well as the orientation sensor. Combining both the location and orientation sensors delivers the global position of the user in the physical world.

The location sensor is mainly supported with a **GNSS (Global Navigation Satellite System)** receiver. One of the most popular GNSS receivers is the GPS (maintained by the USA), which is present on most smartphones.

 Other systems are currently (or will soon be) deployed, such as GLONASS (Russia), Galileo (Europe, 2020), or Compass (China, 2020).

There are several possible orientation sensors available on handheld devices, such as accelerometers, magnetometers, and gyroscopes. The measured position and orientation of your handheld device provides tracking information, which is used for registering virtual objects on the physical scene. The position reported by the GPS module can be both inaccurate and updated slower than you move around. This can result in a **lag,** that is, when you do a fast movement, virtual elements seem to float behind. One of the most popular types of AR applications with sensor-based systems are AR browsers, which visualize **Points of Interests (POIs)**, that is, simple graphical information about things around you. If you try some of the most popular products such as Junaio, Layar, or Wikitude, you will probably observe this effect of lag.

The advantage of this technique is that the sensor-based ARs are working on a general scale around the world, in practically any physical outdoor position (such as if you are in the middle of the desert or in a city). One of the limitations of such systems is their inability to work inside (or work poorly) or in any occluded area (no line-of-sight with the sky, such as in forests or on streets with high buildings all around). We will discuss more about this type of mobile AR system in *Chapter 4, Locating in the World*.

Computer vision-based AR

The other popular type of AR system is computer vision-based AR. The idea here is to leverage the power of the inbuilt camera for more than capturing and displaying the physical world (as done in sensor-based AR). This technology generally operates with image processing and computer vision algorithms that analyze the image to detect any object visible from the camera. This analysis can provide information about the position of different objects and, therefore, the user (more about that in *Chapter 5, Same as Hollywood – Virtual on Physical Objects*).

The advantage is that things seem to be perfectly aligned. The current technology allows you to recognize different types of planar pictorial content, such as a specifically designed marker (**marker-based tracking**) or more natural content (**markerless tracking**). One of the disadvantages is that vision-based AR is heavy in processing and can drain the battery really rapidly. Recent generations of smartphones are more adapted to handle this type of problem, being that they are optimized for energy consumption.

AR architecture concepts

So let's explore how we can support the development of the previously described concepts and the two general AR systems. As in the development of any other application, some well-known concepts of software engineering can be applied in developing an AR application. We will look at the structural aspect of an AR application (software components) followed by the behavioral aspect (control flow).

AR software components

An AR application can be structured in three layers: the application layer, the AR layer, and the OS/Third Party layer.

The **application layer** corresponds to the domain logic of your application. If you want to develop an AR game, anything related to managing the game assets (characters, scenes, objects) or the game logic will be implemented in this specific layer. The AR layer corresponds to the instantiation of the concepts we've previously described. Each of the AR notions and concepts that we've presented (display, registration, and interaction) can be seen, in terms of software, as a modular element, a component, or a service of the AR layer.

You can note that we have separated tracking from registration in the figure, making tracking one major software component for an AR application. Tracking, which provides spatial information to the registration service, is a complex and computationally intensive process in any AR application. The OS/Third Party layer corresponds to existing tools and libraries which don't provide any AR functionalities, but will enable the AR layer. For example, the **Display** module for a mobile application will communicate with the OS layer to access the camera to create a view of the physical world. On Android, the Google Android API is part of this layer. Some additional libraries, such as JMonkeyEngine, which handle the graphics, are also part of this layer.

In the rest of the book, we will show you how to implement the different modules of the AR layer, which also involves communication with the OS/Third Party layer. The major layers of an AR application (see the right-hand side of the following figure), with their application modules (the left-hand side of the following figure), are depicted in the following figure:

Application Logic		Application Layer
Interaction		
Registration		AR Layer
Display	Tracking	
Graphics	Sensors	OS/Third Party Layer
Screen	Camera	

AR control flow

With the concept of software layers and components in mind, we can now look at how information will flow in a typical AR application. We will focus here on describing how each of the components of the AR layer relate to each other over time and what their connections with the OS/Third Party layer are.

Over the last decade, AR researchers and developers have converged toward a well-used method of combining these components using a similar order of execution—the AR control flow. We present here the general AR control flow used by the community and summarized in the following figure:

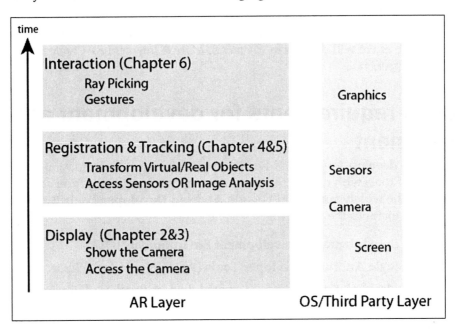

The preceding figure, read from the bottom up, shows the main activities of an AR application. This sequence is repeated indefinitely in an AR application; it can be seen as the typical **AR main loop** (please note that we've excluded the domain logic here as well as the OS activities). Each activity corresponds to the same module we've presented before. The structure of the AR layer and AR control flow is, therefore, quite symmetric.

Understand that this control flow is the key to developing an AR application, so we will come back to it and use it in the rest of the book. We will get into more details of each of the components and steps in the next chapter.

So, looking at the preceding figure, the main activities and steps in your application are as follows:

- **Manage the display first**: For mobile AR, this means accessing the video camera and showing a captured image on the screen (a view of your physical world). We will discuss that in *Chapter 2, Viewing the World*. This also involves matching camera parameters between the physical camera and the virtual one that renders your digital objects (*Chapter 3, Superimposing the World*).

- **Register and track your objects**: Analyze the sensors on your mobile (approach 1) or analyze the video image (approach 2) and detect the position of each element of your world (such as camera or objects). We will discuss this aspect in *Chapter 4, Locating in the World* and *Chapter 5, Same as Hollywood – Virtual on Physical Objects*.

- **Interact**: Once your content is correctly registered, you can start to interact with it, as we will discuss in *Chapter 6, Make It Interactive – Create the User Experience*.

System requirements for development and deployment

If you want to develop Augmented Reality applications for Android, you can share the majority of tools with regular Android developers. Specifically, you can leverage the power of the widely supported **Google Android Developer Tools Bundle (ADT Bundle)**. This includes the following:

- The Eclipse **Integrated Development Environment (IDE)**
- The **Google Android Developer Tools (ADT)** plugin for Eclipse
- The Android platform for your targeted devices (further platforms can be downloaded)
- The Android Emulator with the latest system image

Besides this standard package common to many Android development environments, you will need the following:

- A snapshot of **JMonkeyEngine (JME)**, version 3 or higher
- **Qualcomm® Vuforia™ SDK (Vuforia™)**, version 2.6 or higher
- **Android Native Development Kit (Android NDK)**, version r9 or higher

The JME Java OpenGL® game engine is a free toolkit that brings the 3D graphics in your programs to life. It provides 3D graphics and gaming middleware that frees you from exclusively coding in low-level **OpenGL® ES (OpenGL® for Embedded Systems)**, for example, by providing an asset system for importing models, predefined lighting, and physics and special effects components.

The Qualcomm® Vuforia™ SDK brings state-of-the art computer vision algorithms targeted at recognizing and tracking a wide variety of objects, including fiducials (frame markers), image targets, and even 3D objects. While it is not needed for sensor-based AR, it allows you to conveniently implement computer vision-based AR applications.

The Google Android NDK is a toolset for performance-critical applications. It allows parts of the application to be written in native-code languages (C/C++). While you don't need to code in C or C++, this toolset is required by Vuforia™ SDK.

Of course, you are not bound to a specific IDE and can work with command-line tools as well. The code snippets themselves, which we present in this book, do not rely on the use of a specific IDE. However, within this book, we will give you setup instructions specifically for the popular Eclipse IDE. Furthermore, all development tools can be used on Windows (XP or later), Linux, and Mac OS X (10.7 or later).

On the next pages, we will guide you through the installation processes of the Android Developer Tools Bundle, NDK, JME, and Vuforia™ SDK. While the development tools can be spread throughout the system, we recommend that you use a common base directory for both the development tools and the sample code; let's call it `AR4Android` (for example, `C:/AR4Android` under Windows or `/opt/AR4Android` under Linux or Mac OS X).

Installing the Android Developer Tools Bundle and the Android NDK

You can install the ADT Bundle in two easy steps as follows:

1. Download the ADT Bundle from `http://developer.android.com/sdk/index.html`.

2. After downloading, unzip `adt-bundle-<os_platform>.zip` into the `AR4Android` base directory.

You can then start the Eclipse IDE by launching `AR4Android/adt-bundle-<os_platform>/eclipse/eclipse(.exe)`.

> Please note that you might need to install additional system images, depending on the devices you use (for example, version 2.3.5, or 4.0.1). You can follow the instructions given at the following website: `http://developer.android.com/tools/help/sdk-manager.html`.

For the Android NDK (version r9 or higher), you follow a similar procedure as follows:

1. Download it from `http://developer.android.com/tools/sdk/ndk/index.html`.

2. After downloading, unzip `android-ndk-r<version>Y-<os_platform>.(zip|bz2)` into the `AR4Android` base directory.

Installing JMonkeyEngine

JME is a powerful Java-based 3D game engine. It comes with its own development environment (JME IDE based on NetBeans) which is targeted towards the development of desktop games. While the JME IDE also supports the deployment of Android devices, it (at the time this book is being written) lacks the integration of convenient Android SDK tools like the **Android Debug Bridge (adb)**, **Dalvik Debug Monitor Server view (DDMS)** or integration of the Android Emulator found in the ADT Bundle. So, instead of using the JME IDE, we will integrate the base libraries into our AR projects in Eclipse. The easiest way to obtain the JME libraries is to download the SDK for your operating system from http://jmonkeyengine.org/downloads and install it into the AR4Android base directory (or your own developer directory; just make sure you can easily access it later in your projects). At the time this book is being published, there are three packages: Windows, GNU/Linux, and Mac OS X.

You can also obtain most recent versions from
http://updates.jmonkeyengine.org/nightly/3.0/engine/

You need only the Java libraries of JME (.jar) for the AR development, using the ADT Bundle. If you work on Windows or Linux, you can include them in any existing Eclipse project by performing the following steps:

1. Right-click on your AR project (which we will create in the next chapter) or any other project in the Eclipse explorer and go to **Build Path | Add External Archives**.

2. In the **JAR selection** dialog, browse to AR4Android/jmonkeyplatform/ jmonkeyplatform/libs.

3. You can select **all JARs** in the lib directory and click on **Open**.

If you work on Mac OS X, you should extract the libraries from jmonkeyplatform. app before applying the same procedure as for Windows or Linux described in the preceding section. To extract the libraries, you need to right-click on your jmonkeyplatform.app app and select **Show Package contents** and you will find the libraries in /Applications/jmonkeyplatform.app/Contents/Resources/.

Please note that, in the context of this book, we only use a few of them. In the Eclipse projects accompanying the source code of the book, you will find the necessary JARs already in the local lib directories containing the subset of Java libraries necessary for running the examples. You can also reference them in your build path.

The reference documentation for using JME with Android can be found at `http://hub.jmonkeyengine.org/wiki/doku.php/jme3:android`.

Installing Vuforia™

Vuforia™ is a state-of-the-art library for computer vision recognition and natural feature tracking.

In order to download and install Vuforia™, you have to initially register at `https://developer.vuforia.com/user/register`. Afterwards, you can download the SDK (for Windows, Linux, or Mac OS X) from `https://developer.vuforia.com/resources/sdk/android`. Create a folder named `AR4Android/ThirdParty`. Now create an Eclipse project by going to **File** | **New** | **Project ...** named `ThirdParty` and choose as location the folder `AR4Android/ThirdParty` (see also the section *Creating an Eclipse project* in *Chapter 2, Viewing the World*). Then install the Vuforia™ SDK in `AR4Android/ThirdParty/vuforia-sdk-android-<VERSION>`. For the examples in *Chapter 5, Same as Hollywood – Virtual on Physical Objects* and *Chapter 6, Make It Interactive – Create the User Experience*, you will need to reference this `ThirdParty Eclipse` project.

Which Android devices should you use?

The Augmented Reality applications which you will learn to build will run on a wide variety of Android-powered smartphone and tablet devices. However, depending on the specific algorithms, we will introduce certain hardware requirements that should be met. Specifically, the Android device needs to have the following features:

- A back-facing camera for all examples in this book
- A GPS module for the sensor-based AR examples
- A gyroscope or linear accelerometers for the sensor-based AR examples

Augmented Reality on mobile phones can be challenging as many integrated sensors have to be active during the running of applications and computationally demanding algorithms are executed. Therefore, we recommend deploying them on a dual-core processor (or more cores) for the best AR experience. The earliest Android version to deploy should be 2.3.3 (API 10, Gingerbread). This gives potential outreach to your AR app across approximately 95 percent of all Android devices.

 Visit `http://developer.android.com/about/dashboards/index.html` for up-to-date numbers.

Please make sure to set up your device for development as described at `http://developer.android.com/tools/device.html`.

In addition, most AR applications, specifically the computer-vision based applications (using Vuforia™), require enough processing power.

Summary

In this chapter, we introduced the foundational background of AR. We've presented some of the main concepts of AR, such as sensory augmentation, dedicated display technology, real-time spatial registration of physical and digital information, and interaction with the content.

We've also presented computer vision-based and sensor-based AR systems, the two major trends of architecture on mobile devices. The basic software architecture blocks of an AR application have also been described and will be used as a guide for the remaining presentation of this book. By now, you should have installed the third-party tools used in the coming chapters. In the next chapter, you will get started with viewing the virtual world and implementing camera access with JME.

2
Viewing the World

In this chapter, we will learn how to develop the first element of any mobile AR application: *the view of the real world*. To understand the concept of the view of the real world, we will take a look at the camera application you have installed on your mobile. Open any photo capture application (camera app) you have preinstalled on your android device, or you may have downloaded from the Google Play store (such as Camera Zoom FX, Vignette, and so on). What you can see on the viewfinder of the application is a real-time video stream captured by the camera and displayed on your screen.

If you move the device around while running the application, it seems like you were seeing the real world "through" the device. Actually, the camera seems to act like the eye of the device, perceiving the environment around you. This process is also used for mobile AR development to create a view of the real world. It's the concept of see-through video that we introduced in the previous chapter.

The display of the real world requires two main steps:

- Capturing an image from the camera (camera access)
- Displaying this image on the screen using a graphics library (camera display in JME)

This process is generally repeated in an infinite loop, creating the *real-time* aspect of the view of the physical world. In this chapter, we will discuss how to implement both of these techniques using two different graphics libraries: a low-level one (Android library) and a high-end one (JME 3D scene graph library). While the Android library allows you to quickly display the camera image, it is not designed to be combined with 3D graphics, which you want to augment on the video stream. Therefore, you will implement the camera display also using the JME library. We will also introduce challenges and hints for handling a variety of Android smartphones and their inbuilt cameras.

Understanding the camera

Phone manufacturers are always competing to equip your smartphone with the most advanced camera sensor, packing it with more features, such as higher resolution, better contrast, faster video capture, new autofocus mode, and so on. The consequence is that the capabilities (features) of the mobile phone cameras can differ significantly between smartphone models or brands. Thankfully, the Google Android API provides a generic wrapper for the underlying camera hardware unifying the access for the developer: the Android camera API. For your development, an efficient access to the camera needs a clear understanding of the camera capabilities (parameters and functions) available through the API. Underestimating this aspect will result in slow-running applications or pixelated images, affecting the user experience of your application.

Camera characteristics

Cameras on smartphones nowadays share many characteristics with digital point-and-shoot cameras. They generally support two operative modes: the still image mode (which is an instantaneous, singular capture of an image), or the video mode (which is a continuous, real-time capture of images).

Video and image modes differ in terms of capabilities: an image capture always has, for example, a higher resolution (more pixels) than video. While modern smartphones can easily achieve 8 megapixel in the still image mode, the video mode is restricted to 1080p (about 2 megapixels). In AR, we use the video mode in typically lower resolutions such as VGA (640 x 480) for efficiency reasons. Unlike a standard digital camera, we don't store any content on an external memory card; we just display the image on the screen. This mode has a special name in the Android API: the preview mode.

Some of the common settings (parameters) of the preview mode are:

- **Resolution**: It is the size of the captured image, which can be displayed on your screen. This is also called the size in the Android camera API. Resolution is defined in pixels in terms of width (x) and height (y) of the image. The ratio between them is called the **aspect ratio**, which gives a sense of how square an image is similar to TV resolution (such as 1:1, 4:3, or 16:9).
- **Frame rate**: It defines how fast an image can be captured. This is also called **Frames Per Second (FPS)**.
- **White balance**: It determines what will be the white color on your image, mainly dependent on your environment light (for example, daylight for outdoor situation, incandescent at your home, fluorescent at your work, and so on).

- **Focus**: It defines which part of the image will appear sharp and which part will not be easily discernible (out of focus). Like any other camera, smartphone cameras also support autofocus mode.

- **Pixel format**: The captured image is converted to a specific image format, where the color (and luminance) of each pixel is stored under a specific format. The pixel format not only defines the type of color channels (such as RGB versus YCbCr), but also the storage size of each component (for example, 5, 8, or 16 bits). Some popular pixel formats are RGB888, RGB565, or YCbCr422. In the following figure, you can see common camera parameters, moving from the left to right: image resolution, frame rate for capturing image streams, focus of the camera, the pixel format for storing the images and the white balance:

Other important settings related to the camera workflow are:

- **Playback control**: Defines when you can start, pause, stop, or get the image content of your camera.

- **Buffer control**: A captured image is copied into the memory to be accessible to your application. There are different ways to store this image, for example, using a buffering system.

Configuring these settings correctly is the basic requirement for an AR application. While popular camera apps use only the preview mode for capturing a video or an image, the preview mode is the basis for the view of the real world in AR. Some of the things you need to remember for configuring these camera parameters are:

- The higher the resolution, the lower will be your frame rate, which means your application might look prettier if things do not move fast in the image, but will run more slowly. In contrast, you can have an application running fast but your image will look "blocky" (pixelated effect).

- If the white balance is not set properly, the appearance of digital models overlaid on the video image will not match and the AR experience will be diminished.

- If the focus changes all the time (autofocus), you may not be able to analyze the content of the image and the other components of your application (such as tracking) may not work correctly.

- Cameras on mobile devices use compressed image formats and typically do not offer the same performance as high-end desktop webcams. When you combine your video image (often in RGB565 with 3D rendered content using RGB8888), you might notice the color differences between them.

- If you are doing heavy processing on your image, that can create a delay in your application. Additionally, if your application runs multiple processes concurrently, synchronizing your image capture process with the other processes is rather important.

We advise you to:

- Acquire and test a variety of Android devices and their cameras to get a sense of the camera capabilities and performances.

- Find a compromise between the resolution and frame rate. Standard resolution/frame rate combination used on desktop AR is 640 x 480 at 30 fps. Use it as a baseline for your mobile AR application and optimize from there to get a higher quality AR application for newer devices.

- Optimize the white balance if your AR application is only supposed to be run in a specific environment such as in daylight for an outdoor application.

- Controlling the focus has been one of the limiting aspects of Android smartphones (always on autofocus or configuration not available). Privilege a fixed focus over an autofocus, and optimize the focus range if you are developing a tabletop or room AR application (near focus) versus an outdoor AR application (far focus).

- Experiment with pixel formats, to get the best match with your rendered content.

- Try to use an advanced buffering system, if available, on your target device.

There are other major characteristics of the camera that are not available through the API (or only on some handheld devices), but are important to be considered during the development of your AR application. They are field of view, exposure time, and aperture.

We will only discuss one of them here: the field of view. The field of view corresponds to how much the camera sees from the real world, such as how much your eyes can see from left to right and top to bottom (human vision is around 120 degrees with a binocular vision). The field of view is measured in degrees, and varies largely between cameras (15 degrees to 60 degrees without distortion).

The larger your field of view is, the more you will capture the view of the real world and the better will be the experience. The field of view is dependent on the hardware characteristics of your camera (the sensor size and the focal length of the length). Estimating this field of view can be done with additional tools; we will explore this later on.

Camera versus screen characteristics

The camera and screen characteristics are generally not exactly the same on your mobile platform. The camera image can be, for example, larger than the screen resolution. The aspect ratio of the screen can also differ for one of the cameras. This is a technical challenge in AR as you want to find the best method to fit your camera image on the screen, to create a sense of AR display. You want to maximize the amount of information by putting as much of the camera image on your screen as possible. In the movie industry, they have a similar problem as the recorded format may differ from the playing media (for example, the cinemascope film on your 4:3 mobile device, the 4K movie resolution on your 1080p TV screen, and so on). To address this problem, you can use two fullscreen methods known as stretching and cropping, as shown in the following figure:

Stretching will adapt the camera image to the screen characteristics, at the risk of deforming the original format of the image (mainly its aspect ratio). Cropping will select a subarea of the image to be displayed and you will lose information (it basically zooms into the image until the whole screen is filled). Another approach will be to change the scale of your image, so that one dimension (width or height) of the screen and the image are the same. Here, the disadvantage is that you will lose the fullscreen display of your camera image (a black border will appear on the side of your image). None of the techniques are optimal, so you need to experiment what is more convenient for your application and your target devices.

Accessing the camera in Android

To start with, we will create a simple camera activity to get to know the principles of camera access in Android. While there are convenient Android applications that provide quick means for snapping a picture or recording a video through Android intents, we will get our hands dirty and use the Android camera API to get a customized camera access for our first application.

We will guide you, step-by-step, in creating your first app showing a live camera preview. This will include:

- Creating an Eclipse project
- Requesting relevant permissions in the Android Manifest file
- Creating SurfaceView to be able to capture the preview frames of the camera
- Creating an activity that displays the camera preview frames
- Setting camera parameters

Downloading the example code

You can download the example code files for all Packt books you have purchased from your account at `http://www.packtpub.com`. If you purchased this book elsewhere, you can visit `http://www.packtpub.com/support` and register to have the files e-mailed directly to you. You can also find the code files at `https://github.com/arandroidbook/ar4android`.

Creating an Eclipse project

Our first step is the setup process for creating an Android project in Eclipse. We will call our first project `CameraAccessAndroid`. Please note that the description of this subsection will be similar for all other examples that we will present in this book.

Start your Eclipse project and go to **File | New | Android Application Project**. In the following configuration dialog box, please fill in the appropriate fields as shown in the following screenshot:

Then, click on two more dialog boxes (**Configure Project** for selecting the file path to your project, **Launcher Icon**) by accepting the default values. Then, in the **Create Activity** dialog box, select the **Create Activity** checkbox and the **BlankActivity** option. In the following **New Blank Activity** dialog, fill into the **Activity Name** textbox, for example, with `CameraAccessAndroidActivity` and leave the **Layout Name** textbox to its default value. Finally, click on the **Finish** button and your project should be created and be visible in the project explorer.

Permissions in the Android manifest

For every AR application we will create, we will use the camera. With the Android API, you explicitly need to allow camera access in the Android manifest declaration of your application. In the top-level folder of your `CameraAccessAndroid` project, open the `AndroidManifest.xml` file in the text view. Then add the following permission:

```
<uses-permission android:name="android.permission.CAMERA" />
```

Besides this permission, the application also needs to at least declare the use of camera features:

```
<uses-feature android:name="android.hardware.camera" />
```

Since we want to run the AR application in fullscreen mode (for better immersion), add the following option into the activity tag:

```
android:theme="@android:style/Theme.NoTitleBar.Fullscreen"
```

Creating an activity that displays the camera

In its most basic form, our `Activity` class takes care of setting up the `Camera` instance. As a class member, you need to declare an instance of a `Camera` class:

```
public class CameraAccessAndroidActivity extends Activity {
private Camera mCamera;

}
```

The next step is to open the camera. To do that, we define a `getCameraInstance()` method:

```
public static Camera getCameraInstance() {
  Camera c = null;
  try {
    c = Camera.open(0);
  } catch (Exception e) { ...  }
  return c;
}
```

It is important that the `open()` call is surrounded by `try{}catch{}` blocks as the camera might currently be used by other processes and be unavailable. This method is called in the `onResume()` method of your `Activity` class:

```
public void onResume() {
  super.onResume();
  stopPreview = false;
  mCamera = getCameraInstance();
  ...
}
```

It is also crucial to properly release the camera when you pause or exit your program. Otherwise it will be blocked if you open another (or the same) program. We define a `releaseCamera()` method for this:

```
private void releaseCamera() {
  if (mCamera != null) {

    mCamera.release();
    mCamera = null;
  }
}
```

You then call this method in the `onPause()` method of your `Activity` class.

 On some devices, it can be slow to open the camera. In this case, you can use an `AsyncTask` class to mitigate the problem.

Setting camera parameters

You now have a basic workflow to start and stop your camera. The Android camera API also allows you to query and set various camera parameters that were discussed at the beginning of this chapter. Specifically, you should be careful not to use very high resolution images as they take a lot of processing power. For a typical mobile AR application, you do not want to have a higher video resolution of 640 x 480 (VGA).

As camera modules can be quite different, it is not advisable to hardcode the video resolution. Instead, it is a good practice to query the available resolutions of your camera sensor and only use the most optimal resolution for your application, if it is supported.

Let's say, you have predefined the video width you want in the mDesiredCameraPreviewWidth variable. You can then check if the value of the width resolution (and an associated video height) is supported by the camera using the following method:

```
private void initializeCameraParameters() {
  Camera.Parameters parameters = mCamera.getParameters();
  List<Camera.Size> sizes = parameters.getSupportedPreviewSizes();
  int currentWidth = 0;
  int currentHeight = 0;
  boolean foundDesiredWidth = false;
  for(Camera.Size s: sizes) {
    if (s.width == mDesiredCameraPreviewWidth)  {
      currentWidth = s.width;
      currentHeight = s.height;
      foundDesiredWidth = true;
      break;
    }
  }
  if(foundDesiredWidth)
    parameters.setPreviewSize( currentWidth, currentHeight );
  mCamera.setParameters(parameters);
}
```

The mCamera.getParameters() method is used to query the current camera parameters. The mCamera.getParameters() and getSupportedPreviewSizes() methods return the subset of available preview sizes and the parameters. setPreviewSize method is setting the new preview size. Finally, you have to call the mCamera.setParameters(parameters) method so that the requested changes are implemented. This initializeCameraParameters() method can then also be called in the onResume() method of your Activity class.

Creating SurfaceView

For your Augmented Reality application, you want to display a stream of live images from your back-facing camera on the screen. In a standard application, acquiring the video and displaying the video are two independent procedures. With the Android API, you explicitly need to have a separate SurfaceView to display the camera stream as well. The SurfaceView class is a dedicated drawing area that you can embed into your application.

So for our example, we need to derive a new class from the Android `SurfaceView` class (lets call it `CameraPreview`) and implement a `SurfaceHolder.Callback` interface. This interface is used to react to any events related to the surface, such as the creation, change, and destruction of the surface. Accessing the mobile camera is done through the `Camera` class. In the constructor, the Android `Camera` instance (defined previously) is passed:

```
public class CameraPreview extends SurfaceView implements
   SurfaceHolder.Callback {
   private static final String TAG = "CameraPreview";
   private SurfaceHolder mHolder;
   private Camera mCamera;
   public CameraPreview(Context context, Camera camera) {
     super(context);
     mCamera = camera;
     mHolder = getHolder();
     mHolder.addCallback(this);
     mHolder.setType(SurfaceHolder.SURFACE_TYPE_PUSH_BUFFERS);
   }
```

In the `surfaceChanged` method, you take care of passing an initialized `SurfaceHolder` instance (that is the instance that holds the display surface) and starting the preview stream of the camera, which you later want to display (and process) in your own application. The stopping of the camera preview stream is important as well:

```
public void surfaceChanged(SurfaceHolder holder, int format,
   int w, int h) {
   if (mHolder.getSurface() == null){
     return;
   }
   try {
     mCamera.stopPreview();
   } catch (Exception e){ ...}
   try {
     mCamera.setPreviewDisplay(mHolder);
     mCamera.startPreview();
   } catch (Exception e){ ... }
}
```

The inherited methods, `surfaceCreated()` and `surfaceDestroyed()`, remain empty.

Having our `CameraPreview` class defined, we can declare it in the `Activity` class:

```
private CameraPreview mPreview;
```

Then, instantiate it in the `onResume()` method:

```
mPreview = new CameraPreview(this, mCamera);
setContentView(mPreview);
```

To test your application, you can do the same with your other project: please connect your testing device to your computer via a USB cable. In Eclipse, right-click on your project folder, `CameraAccessAndroid`, and in the pop-up menu go to **Run As | 1 Android Application**. You should now be able to see the live camera view on your mobile screen as soon as the application is uploaded and started.

Live camera view in JME

In the preceding example, you got a glimpse of how you can access the Android camera with a low-level graphics library (standard Android library). Since we want to perform Augmented Reality, we will need to have another technique to overlay the virtual content over the video view. There are different ways to do that, and the best method is certainly to use a common view, which will integrate the virtual and video content nicely. A powerful technique is to use a managed 3D graphics library based on a scenegraph model. A scenegraph is basically a data structure that helps you to build elaborate 3D scenes more easily than in plain OpenGL® by logically organizing basic building blocks, such as geometry or spatial transformations. As you installed JME in the first chapter, we will use this specific library offering all the characteristics we need for our AR development. In this subsection, we will explore how you can use JME to display the video. Different to our preceding example, the camera view will be integrated to the 3D scenegraph. In order to achieve this, you use the following steps:

1. Create a project with JME support.
2. Create the activity which sets up JME.
3. Create the JME application, which does the actual rendering of our 3D scene.

For creating the project with JME, you can follow the instructions in the *Installing JMonkeyEngine* section of *Chapter 1, Augmented Reality Concepts and Tools*. We will make a new project called `CameraAccessJME`.

Creating the JME activity

As an Android developer, you know that an Android activity is the main entry point to create your applications. However, JME is a platform-independent game engine that runs on many platforms with Java support. The creators of JME wanted to ease the process of integrating existing (and new) JME applications into Android as easily as possible. Therefore, they explicitly differentiated between the JME applications, which do the actual rendering of the scene (and could be used on other platforms as well), and the Android specific parts in the JME activity for setting up the environment to allow the JME application to run. The way they achieved this is to have a specific class called `AndroidHarness`, which takes the burden off the developer to configure the Android activity properly. For example, it maps touch events on your screen to mouse events in the JME application. One challenge in this approach is to forward Android-specific events, which are not common to other platforms in the JME application. Don't worry, we will show you how to do this for the camera images.

The first thing you want to do is create an Android activity derived from the `AndroidHarness` class, which we will call the `CameraAccessJMEActivity` method. Just like the `CameraAccessAndroidActivity` class, it holds instances of the `Camera` and `CameraPreview` classes. In contrast, it will also hold an instance of your actual JME application (discussed in the next section of this chapter) responsible for rendering your scene. You did not yet provide an actual instance of the class but only the fully qualified path name. The instance of your class is constructed at runtime through a reflection technique in the `AndroidHarness` super class:

```
public CameraAccessJMEActivity() {
    appClass = "com.ar4android.CameraAccessJME";
}
```

During runtime, you can then access the actual instance by casting a general JME application class, which `AndroidHarness` stores in its `app` variable to your specific class, for example, through the `(com.ar4android.CameraAccessJME)` app.

As discussed at the beginning of this chapter, the camera can deliver the images in various pixel formats. Most rendering engines (and JME is no exception) cannot handle the wide variety of pixel formats but expect certain formats such as RGB565. The RGB565 format stores the red and blue components in 5 bits and the green component in 6 bits, thereby displaying 65536 colors in 16 bits per pixel. You can check if your camera supports this format in the `initializeCameraParameters` method by adding the following code:

```
List<Integer> pixelFormats =
    parameters.getSupportedPreviewFormats();
    for (Integer format : pixelFormats) {
```

```
    if (format == ImageFormat.RGB_565) {
      pixelFormatConversionNeeded = false;
      parameters.setPreviewFormat(format);
      break;
    }
  }
}
```

In this code snippet, we query all available pixel formats (iterating over `parameters.getSupportedPreviewFormats()`) and set the pixel format of the RGB565 model if supported (and remember that we did this by setting the flag `pixelFormatConversionNeeded`).

As mentioned before, in contrast to the previous example, we will not directly render the `SurfaceView` class. Instead, we will copy the preview images from the camera in each frame. To prepare for this, we define the `preparePreviewCallbackBuffer()` method, which you will call in the `onResume()` method after creating your camera and setting its parameters. It allocates buffers to copy the camera images and forwarding it to JME:

```
public void preparePreviewCallbackBuffer() {

  mPreviewWidth = mCamera.getParameters().getPreviewSize().width;
  mPreviewHeight = mCamera.getParameters().
    getPreviewSize().height;
  int bufferSizeRGB565 = mPreviewWidth * mPreviewHeight * 2 +
    4096;
  mPreviewBufferRGB565 = null;
  mPreviewBufferRGB565 = new byte[bufferSizeRGB565];
  mPreviewByteBufferRGB565 =
    ByteBuffer.allocateDirect(mPreviewBufferRGB565.length);
  cameraJMEImageRGB565 = new Image(Image.Format.RGB565,
    mPreviewWidth, mPreviewHeight, mPreviewByteBufferRGB565);
}
```

If your camera does not support RGB565, it may deliver the frame in the YCbCr format (Luminance, blue difference, red difference), which you have to convert to the RGB565 format. To do that, we will use a color space conversion method, which is really common in AR and for image processing. We provide an implementation of this method (`yCbCrToRGB565(...)`) available in the sample project. A basic approach to use this method is to create different image buffers, where you will copy the source, intermediate, and final transformed image.

So for the conversion, the `mPreviewWidth`, `mPreviewHeight`, and `bitsPerPixel` variables are queried by calling the `getParameters()` method of your camera instance in the `preparePreviewCallbackBuffer()` method and determine the size of your byte arrays holding the image data. You will pass a JME image (`cameraJMEImageRGB565`) to the JME application, which is constructed from a Java `ByteBuffer` class, which itself just wraps the RGB565 byte array.

Having prepared the image buffers, we now need to access the content of the actual image. In Android, you do this by an implementation of the `Camera.PreviewCallback` interface. In the `onPreviewFrame(byte[] data, Camera c)` method of this object, you can get access to the actual camera image stored as a byte array:

```
private final Camera.PreviewCallback mCameraCallback = new
  Camera.PreviewCallback() {
    public void onPreviewFrame(byte[] data, Camera c) {

      mPreviewByteBufferRGB565.clear();
      if (pixelFormatConversionNeeded) {
        yCbCrToRGB565(data, mPreviewWidth, mPreviewHeight,
          mPreviewBufferRGB565);
        mPreviewByteBufferRGB565.put(mPreviewBufferRGB565);
      }

      cameraJMEImageRGB565.setData(mPreviewByteBufferRGB565);
      if ((com.ar4android.CameraAccessJME) app != null) {
        ((com.ar4android.CameraAccessJME)
          app).setTexture(cameraJMEImageRGB565);
      }

    }
  }
```

The `setTexture` method of the `CameraAccessJME` class simply copies the incoming data into a local image object.

Finally, you register your implementation of the `Camera.PreviewCallback` interface in the `onSurfaceChanged()` method of the `CameraPreview` class:

```
mCamera.setPreviewCallback(mCameraPreviewCallback);
```

A faster method to retrieve the camera images, which avoids creating a new buffer in each frame, is to allocate a buffer before and use it with the methods, `mCamera.addCallbackBuffer()` and `mCamera.setPreviewCallbackWithBuffer()`. Please note that this approach might be incompatible with some devices.

Creating the JME application

As mentioned in the preceding section, the JME application is the place where the actual rendering of the scene takes place. It should not concern itself with the nitty-gritty details of the Android system, which were described earlier. JME provides you with a convenient way to initialize your application with many default settings. All you have to do is inherit from the `SimpleApplication` class, initialize your custom variables in `simpleInitApp()`, and eventually update them before a new frame is rendered in the `simpleUpdate()` method. For our purpose of rendering the camera background, we will create a custom `ViewPort` (a view inside the display window), and a virtual `Camera` (for rendering the observed scene), in the `initVideoBackground` method. The common method to display the video in a scene graph such as JME is to use the video image as a texture, which is placed on a quadrilateral mesh:

```java
public void initVideoBackground(int screenWidth, int screenHeight)
{
  Quad videoBGQuad = new Quad(1, 1, true);
  mVideoBGGeom = new Geometry("quad", videoBGQuad);
  float newWidth = 1.f * screenWidth / screenHeight;
  mVideoBGGeom.setLocalTranslation(-0.5f * newWidth, -0.5f, 0.f);
  mVideoBGGeom.setLocalScale(1.f * newWidth, 1.f, 1);
  mvideoBGMat = new Material(assetManager,
    "Common/MatDefs/Misc/Unshaded.j3md");
  mVideoBGGeom.setMaterial(mvideoBGMat);
  mCameraTexture = new Texture2D();

  Camera videoBGCam = cam.clone();
  videoBGCam.setParallelProjection(true);
  ViewPort videoBGVP = renderManager.createMainView("VideoBGView",
    videoBGCam);
  videoBGVP.attachScene(mVideoBGGeom);
  mSceneInitialized = true;
}
```

Let's have a more detailed look at this essential method for setting up our scenegraph for the rendering of the video background. You first create a quad shape and assign it to a JME `Geometry` object. To assure correct mapping between the screen and the camera, you scale and reposition the geometry according to the dimensions of the device's screen. You assign a material to the quad and also create a texture for it. Since we are doing 3D rendering, we need to define the camera looking at this quad. As we want the camera to only see the quad nicely placed in front of the camera without distortion, we create a custom viewport and an orthographic camera (this orthographic camera has no perspective foreshortening). Finally, we add the quad geometry to this viewport.

Now, we have our camera looking at the textured quad rendered fullscreen. All that is left to do is update the texture of the quad each time a new video frame is available from the camera. We will do this in the `simpleUpdate()` method, which is called regularly by the JME rendering engine:

```
public void simpleUpdate(float tpf) {
if(mNewCameraFrameAvailable) {
  mCameraTexture.setImage(mCameraImage);
  mvideoBGMat.setTexture("ColorMap", mCameraTexture)
}

}
```

You may have noted the usage of the conditional test on the `mNewCameraFrameAvailable` variable. As the scenegraph renders its content with a different refresh rate (up to 60 fps, on a modern smartphone) than what a mobile camera can normally deliver (typically 20-30 fps), we use the `mNewCameraFrameAvailable` flag to only update the texture if a new image becomes available.

So this is it. With these steps implemented, you can compile and upload your application and should get a similar result as shown in the following figure:

Summary

In this chapter you got an introduction to the world of Android camera access and how to display camera images in the JME 3D rendering engine. You learned about various camera parameters and the compromises you have made (for example, between image size and frames per second) to get an efficient camera access. We also introduced the simplest way of displaying a camera view in an Android activity, but also explained why you need to go beyond this simple example to integrate the camera view and 3D graphics in a single application. Finally, we helped you through the implementation of a JME application, which renders the camera background. The knowledge you gained in this chapter is the beneficial basis to overlay the first 3D objects on the camera view—a topic we will discuss in the next chapter.

3

Superimposing the World

Now that you have a view of the physical world on your screen, our next goal is to overlay digital 3D models on top of it. Overlay in 3D as used in Augmented Reality, is different from basic 2D overlays possible with Adobe Photoshop or similar drawing applications (in which we only adjust the position of two 2D layers). The notion of 3D overlay involves the management and rendering of content with six degrees of freedom (translation and rotation in three dimensions) as shown in the following figure:

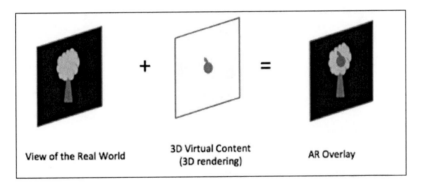

In this chapter, we will guide you through the different concepts and present you with the best way to superimpose real and virtual content. We will successively describe the concept of real and virtual cameras, how to perform superimposition with our scene graph engine, and create high quality superimposition. First, let's discuss the 3D world and the virtual camera.

The building blocks of 3D rendering

Representing and rendering virtual 3D content operates in the same way as when you click a picture with a digital camera in the physical world. If you take a picture of your friend or a landscape, you will first check your subject with the naked eye and after that will look at it through the viewfinder of the camera; only then will you take the picture. These three different steps are the same with virtual 3D content. You do not have a physical camera taking pictures, but you will use a **virtual camera** to render your scene. Your virtual camera can be seen as a digital representation of a real camera and can be configured in a similar way; you can position your camera, change its field of view, and so on. With virtual 3D content, you manipulate a digital representation of a geometrical 3D scene, which we simply call your virtual 3D scene or virtual world.

The three basic steps for rendering a scene using 3D computer graphics are shown in the following figure and consist of:

- Configuring your virtual 3D scene (objects position and appearance)
- Configuring your virtual camera
- Rendering the 3D scene with the virtual camera

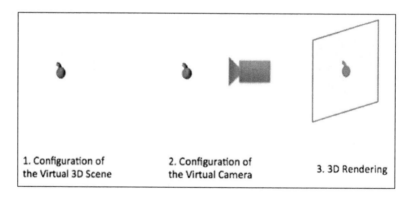

1. Configuration of the Virtual 3D Scene
2. Configuration of the Virtual Camera
3. 3D Rendering

As we do real-time rendering for AR, you will repeat these steps in a loop; objects or cameras can be moved at each time frame (typically at 20-30 FPS).

While positioning objects in a scene, or the camera in a scene, we need a way of representing the location (and also the orientation) of objects as functions of each other. To do so, we generally use some spatial representation of the scene based on geometric mathematical models. The most common approach is to use **Euclidian geometry** and **coordinate systems**. A coordinate system defines a method of referencing an object (or point) in a space using a numerical representation to define this position (**coordinates**). Everything in your scene can be defined in a coordinate system, and coordinate systems can be related to each other using **transformations**.

The most common coordinate systems are shown in the following figure and are:

- **World Coordinate System**: It is the ground where you reference everything.

- **Camera Coordinate System**: It is placed in the world coordinate system and used to render your scene seen from this specific viewpoint. It is sometimes also referenced as the Eye Coordinate System.

- **Local Coordinate System(s)**: It is, for example, an object coordinate system, used to represent the 3D points of an object. Traditionally, you use the (geometric) center of your object to define your local coordinate system.

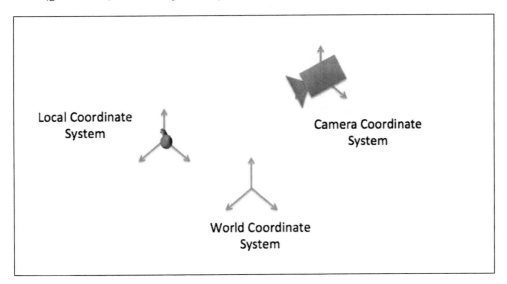

 There are two conventions for the orientation of the coordinate systems: left-handed and right-handed. In both the conventions, X goes on the right-hand side and Y goes upwards. Z goes towards you in the right-handed convention and away from you in the left-handed convention.

Another common coordinate system, not illustrated here, is the image coordinate system. You are probably familiar with this one if you edit your pictures. It defines the position of each pixel of your image from a referenced origin (commonly the top-left corner or the bottom-left corner of an image). When you perform 3D graphics rendering, it's the same concept. Now we will focus on the virtual camera characteristics.

Real camera and virtual camera

A virtual camera for 3D graphics rendering is generally represented by two main sets of parameters: the **extrinsic** and **intrinsic** parameters. The extrinsic parameters define the location of the camera in the virtual world (the transformation from the world coordinate system to the camera coordinate system and vice versa). The intrinsic parameters define the projective properties of the camera, including its field of view (focal length), image center, and skew. Both the parameters can be represented with different data structures, with the most common being a matrix.

If you develop a 3D mobile game, you are generally free to configure the cameras the way you want; you can put the camera above a 3D character running on a terrain (extrinsic) or set up a large field of view to have a large view of the character and the terrain (intrinsic). However, when you do Augmented Reality, the choice is constrained by the properties of the real camera in your mobile phone. In AR, we want properties of the virtual camera to match those of the real camera: the field of view and the camera position. This is an important element of AR, and we will explain how to realize it further in this chapter.

Camera parameters (intrinsic orientation)

The extrinsic parameters of the virtual camera will be explored in subsequent chapters; they are used for 3D registration in Augmented Reality. For our 3D overlay, we will now explore the intrinsic camera parameters.

There are different computational models for representing a virtual camera (and its parameters) and we will use the most popular one: the pinhole camera model. The pinhole camera model is a simplified model of a physical camera, where you consider that there is only a single point (pinhole) where light enters your camera image. With this assumption, computer vision researchers simplify the description of the intrinsic parameters as:

- **Focal length of your (physical or virtual) lens**: This together with the size of the camera center determines the **field of view (FOV)** — also called the angle of view — of your camera. The FOV is the extent of the object space your camera can see and is represented in radians (or degrees). It can be determined for the horizontal, vertical, and diagonal direction of your camera sensor.

- **Image center (principal point)**: This accommodates any displacement of the sensor from the center position.

- **Skew factor**: This is used for non-square pixels.

On non-mobile cameras you should also consider the lens distortion, such as the radial and the tangential distortions. They can be modeled and corrected with advanced software algorithms. Lens distortions on mobile phone cameras are usually corrected in hardware.

With all these concepts in mind, let's do a bit of practice now.

Using the scenegraph to overlay a 3D model onto the camera view

In the previous chapter you learned how to set up a single viewport and camera to render the video background. While the virtual camera determines how your 3D graphics are projected on a 2D image plane, the viewport defines the mapping of this image plane to a part of the actual window in which your application runs (or the whole screen of the smartphone if the app runs in fullscreen mode). It determines the portion of the application window in which graphics are rendered. Multiple viewports can be stacked and can cover the same or different screen areas as shown in the following figure. For a basic AR application, you typically have two viewports. One is associated with the camera rendering the background video and one is used with a camera rendering the 3D objects. Typically, these viewports cover the whole screen.

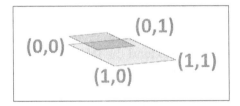

The viewport size is not defined in pixels but is unitless and is defined from 0 to 1 for the width and height to be able to easily adapt to changing window sizes. One camera is associated with one viewport at a time.

Remember that for the video background we used an orthographic camera to avoid perspective foreshortening of the video image. However, this perspective is crucial for getting a proper visual impression of your 3D objects. Orthographic (parallel) projection (on the left-hand side of the following figure) and perspective projection (on the right-hand side of the following figure) determine how the 3D volume is projected on a 2D image plane as shown in the following figure:

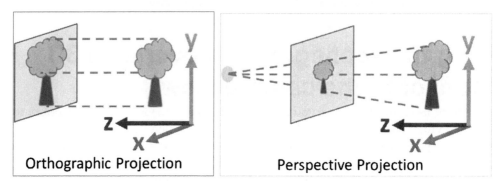

JME uses a right-handed coordinate system (OpenGL® convention, x on the right-hand side, y upwards, and z towards you). You certainly want 3D objects to appear bigger as the camera moves closer to them and smaller as it moves away. So how do we go along? Right, you just add a second camera—this time a perspective one—and an associated viewport that also covers the whole application window.

In the `SuperimposeJME` project associated with this chapter, we again have Android activity (`SuperimposeJMEActivity.java`) and a JME application class (`SuperimposeJME.java`). The application needs no major change from our previous project; you only have to extend the JME `SimpleApplication` class. In its `simpleInitApp()` startup method, we now explicitly differentiate between the initialization of the scene geometry (video background: `initVideoBackground()`; 3D foreground scene: `initForegroundScene()`) and the associated cameras and viewports:

```
private float mForegroundCamFOVY = 30;
...
public void simpleInitApp() {
...
initVideoBackground(settings.getWidth(), settings.getHeight());
initForegroundScene();
initBackgroundCamera();
initForegroundCamera(mForegroundCamFOVY);
...
}
```

Note that the order in which the camera and viewports are initialized is important. Only when we first add the camera and viewport for the video background (initBackgroundCamera()) and later add the foreground camera and viewport (initForegroundCamera()), can we ensure that our 3D objects are rendered on top of the video background; otherwise, you would only see the video background.

We will now add your first 3D model into the scene using initForegroundScene(). A convenient feature of JME is that it supports the loading of external assets—for example, Wavefront files (.obj) or Ogre3D files (.mesh.xml/.scene)—including animations. We will load and animate a green ninja, a default asset that ships with JME.

```java
private AnimControl mAniControl;
private AnimChannel mAniChannel;
...
public void initForegroundScene() {
Spatial ninja = assetManager.loadModel("Models/Ninja/Ninja.mesh.xml");
ninja.scale(0.025f, 0.025f, 0.025f);
ninja.rotate(0.0f, -3.0f, 0.0f);
ninja.setLocalTranslation(0.0f, -2.5f, 0.0f);
rootNode.attachChild(ninja);

DirectionalLight sun = new DirectionalLight();
sun.setDirection(new Vector3f(-0.1f, -0.7f, -1.0f));
rootNode.addLight(sun);

mAniControl = ninja.getControl(AnimControl.class);
mAniControl.addListener(this);
mAniChannel = mAniControl.createChannel();
mAniChannel.setAnim("Walk");
mAniChannel.setLoopMode(LoopMode.Loop);
mAniChannel.setSpeed(1f);
}
```

So in this method you load a model relative to your project's root/asset folder. If you want to load other models, you also place them in this asset folder. You scale, translate, and orient it and then add it to the root scenegraph node. To make the model visible, you also add a directional light shining from the top front onto the model (you can try not adding the light and see the result). For the animation, access the "Walk" animation sequence stored in the model. In order to do this, your class needs to implement the AnimEventListener interface and you need to use an AnimControl instance to access that animation sequence in the model. Finally, you will assign the "Walk" sequence to an AnimChannel instance, tell it to loop the animation, and set the animation speed.

Great, you have now loaded your first 3D model, but you still need to display it on the screen.

This is what you do next in initForegroundCamera(fovY). It takes care of setting up the perspective camera and the associated viewport for your 3D model. As the perspective camera is characterized by the spatial extent of the object space it can see (the FOV), we pass the vertical angle of view stored in mForegroundCamFOVY to the method. It then attaches the root node of our scene containing the 3D model to the foreground viewport.

```
public void initForegroundCamera(float fovY) {
   Camera fgCam = new Camera(settings.getWidth(),
   settings.getHeight());
   fgCam.setLocation(new Vector3f(0f, 0f, 10f));
   fgCam.setAxes(new Vector3f(-1f,0f,0f),
   new Vector3f(0f,1f,0f), new Vector3f(0f,0f,-1f));
   fgCam.setFrustumPerspective(fovY,
   settings.getWidth()/settings.getHeight(), 1, 1000);

   ViewPort fgVP = renderManager.createMainView("ForegroundView",
   fgCam);
   fgVP.attachScene(rootNode);
   fgVP.setBackgroundColor(ColorRGBA.Blue);
   fgVP.setClearFlags(false, true, false);
}
```

While you could just copy some standard parameters from the default camera (similar to what we did with the video background camera), it is good to know which steps you actually have to do to initialize a new camera. After creating a perspective camera initialized with the window width and height, you set both the location (setLocation()) and the rotation (setAxes()) of the camera. JME uses a right-handed coordinate system, and our camera is configured to look along the negative z axis into the origin just as depicted in the previous figure. In addition, we set the vertical angle of the view passed to setFrustumPerspective() to 30 degrees, which corresponds approximately with a field of view that appears natural to a human (as opposed to a very wide or very narrow field of view).

Afterwards, we set up the viewport as we did for the video background camera. In addition, we tell the viewport to delete its depth buffer but retain the color and stencil buffers with setClearFlags(false, true, false). We do this to ensure that our 3D models are always rendered in front of the quadrilateral holding the video texture, no matter if they are actually before or behind that quad in object space (beware that all our graphical objects are referenced in the same world coordinate system). We do not clear the color buffer as, otherwise, the color values of the video background, which are previously rendered into the color buffer will be deleted and we will only see the background color of this viewport (blue). If you run your application now, you should be able to see a walking ninja in front of your video background, as shown in the following pretty cool screenshot:

Improving the overlay

In the previous section you created a perspective camera, which renders your model with a vertical field of view of 30 degrees. However, to increase the realism of your scene, you actually want to match the field of view of your virtual and physical cameras as well as possible. This field of view in a general imaging system such as your phone's camera is dependent both on the size of the camera sensor and the focal length of the optics used. The focal length is a measure of how strongly the camera lens bends incoming parallel light rays until they come into focus (on the sensor plane), it is basically the distance between the sensor plane and the optical elements of your lens.

The FOV can be computed from the formula $a = 2 \arctan d/2f$, where d is the (vertical, horizontal, or diagonal) extent of the camera sensor and 2 is the focal length. Sounds easy, right? There is only a small challenge. You most often do not know the (physical) sensor size or the focal length of the phone camera. The good thing about the preceding formula is that you do not need to know the physical extent of your sensor or its focal length but can calculate it in arbitrary coordinates such as pixels. And for the sensor size, we can easily use the resolution of the camera image, which you already learned to query in *Chapter 2, Viewing the World*.

The trickiest part is to estimate the focal length of your camera. There are some tools that help you to do just this using a set of pictures taken from a known object; they are called camera resectioning tools (or geometric camera calibration tools). We will show you how to achieve this with a tool called GML C++ Camera Calibration Toolbox, which you can download from `http://graphics.cs.msu.ru/en/node/909`.

After installing the tool, open the standard camera app on your Android phone. Under the still image settings select the camera resolution that you also use in your JME application, for example, **640 x 480**, as shown in the following screenshot:

Take an A4 size printout of the `checkerboard_8x5_A4.pdf` file in the GML Calibration pattern subdirectory. Take at least four pictures with your camera app from different viewpoints (6 to 8 pictures will be better). Try to avoid very acute angles and try to maximize the checkerboards in the image. Example images are depicted in the following figure:

When you are done, transfer the images to a folder on your computer (for example, AR4Android\calibration-images). Afterwards, start the GML Camera Calibration app on your computer and create a new project. Type into the **New project** dialog box the correct number of black and white squares (for example, 5 and 8), as shown in the following screenshot:

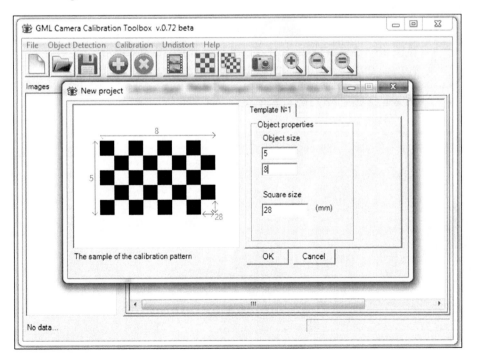

It is also crucial to actually measure the square size as your printer might scale the PDF to its paper size. Then, click on **OK** and start adding the pictures you have just taken (navigate to **Object detection | Add image**). When you have added all the images, navigate to **Object detection | Detect All** and then **Calibration | Calibrate**. If the calibration was successful, you should see camera parameters in the result tab. We are mostly interested in the **Focal length** section. While there are two different focal lengths for the x and y axes, it is fine to just use the first one. In the sample case of the images, which were taken with a Samsung Galaxy SII, the resulting focal length is 522 pixels.

You can then plug this number together with your vertical image resolution into the preceding formula and retrieve the vertical angle of the view in radians. As JME needs the angle in degrees, you simply convert it by applying this factor: *180/PI*. If you are also using a Samsung Galaxy SII, a vertical angle of view of approximately 50 degrees should result, which equals a focal length of approximately 28 mm in 35 mm film format (wide angle lens). If you plug this into the `mForegroundCamFOVY` variable and upload the application, the walking ninja should appear smaller as shown in the following figure. Of course, you can increase its size again by adjusting the camera position.

Note that you cannot model all parameters of the physical camera in JME. For example, you cannot easily set the principal point of your physical camera with your JME camera.

 JME also doesn't support direct lens distortion correction. You can account for these artifacts via advanced lens correction techniques covered, for example, here: `http://paulbourke.net/miscellaneous/lenscorrection/`.

Summary

In this chapter, we introduced you to the concept of 3D rendering, the 3D virtual camera, and the notion of 3D overlay for Augmented Reality. We presented what a virtual camera is and its characteristics and described the importance of intrinsic camera parameters for accurate Augmented Reality. You also got a chance to develop your first 3D overlay and calibrate your mobile camera for improved realism. However, as you move your phone along, the video background changes, while the 3D models stay in place. In the next chapter, we will tackle one of the fundamental bricks of an Augmented Reality application: the registration.

4
Locating in the World

In the last chapter you learned how to overlay digital content on the view of the physical world. However, if you move around with your device, point it somewhere else, the virtual content will always stay at the same place on your screen. This is not exactly what happens in AR. The virtual content should stay at the same place relative to the physical world (and you can move around it), not remaining fixed on your screen.

In this chapter we will look at how to achieve **dynamic registration** between digital content and the physical space. If at every time step, we update the position of moving objects in our application, we will create the feeling that digital content sticks to the physical world. Following the position of moving elements in our scene can be defined as **tracking**, and this is what we will use and implement in this chapter. We will use sensor-based AR to update the registration between digital content and physical space. As some of these sensors are commonly of poor quality, we will show you how to improve the measurement you get from them using a technique named **sensor fusion**. To make it more practical, we will show you how to develop the basic building blocks for a simple prototype of one of the most common AR applications using global tracking: an AR Browser (such as Junaio, Layar, or Wikitude).

Knowing where you are – handling GPS

In this section, we will look at one of the major approaches for mobile AR and sensor-based AR (see *Chapter 1, Augmented Reality Concepts and Tools*), which uses **global tracking**. Global tracking refers to tracking in a global reference frame (world coordinate system), which can encompass the whole earth. We will first look at the position aspect, and then the location sensor built on your phone that will be used for AR. We will learn how to retrieve information from it using the Android API and will integrate its position information into JME.

GPS and GNSS

So we need to track the position of the user to know where he/she is located in the real world. While we say we track the user, handheld AR applications actually track the position of the device.

User tracking versus device tracking

To create a fully-immersive AR application, you ideally need to know where the device is, where the body of the user in reference to the device is, and where the eyes of the user in reference of the body are. This approach has been explored in the past, especially with Head Mounted Displays. For that, you need to track the head of the user, the body of the user, and have all the static transformations between them (calibration). With mobile AR, we are still far from that; maybe in the future, users will wear glasses or clothes equipped with sensors which will allow creating more precise registration and tracking.

So how do we track the position of the device in a global coordinate system? Certainly you, or maybe some of your friends, have used a GPS for car navigation or for going running or hiking. GPS is one example of a common technology used for global tracking, in reference to an earth coordinate system, as shown in the following figure:

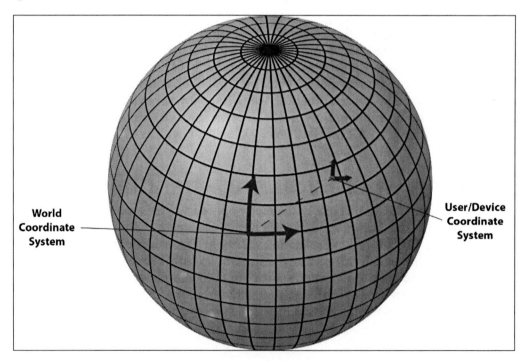

Most mobile phones are now equipped with GPS, so it seems an ideal technology for global tracking in AR. A GPS is the American version of a **global navigation satellite system (GNSS)**. The technology relies on a constellation of geo-referenced satellites, which can give your position anywhere around the planet using geographic coordinates. GPS is not the only GNSS out there; a Russian version (**GLONASS**) is currently also operational, and a European version (**Galileo**) will be effective around 2020. However, GPS is currently the most supported GNSS on mobile devices, so we will use this term for the rest of the book when we talk about tracking with GNSS.

For common AR applications relying on GPS, you have two things to consider: the digital content location and the device location. If both of them are defined in the same coordinate system, in reference to earth, you will be able to know how they are in reference to each other (see the elliptical pattern in the following figure). With that knowledge, you can model the position of the 3D content in the user coordinate system and update it with each location update from your GPS sensor. As a result, if you move closer to an object (bottom to top), the object will appear closer (and bigger in the image), reproducing the behavior you have in the normal world.

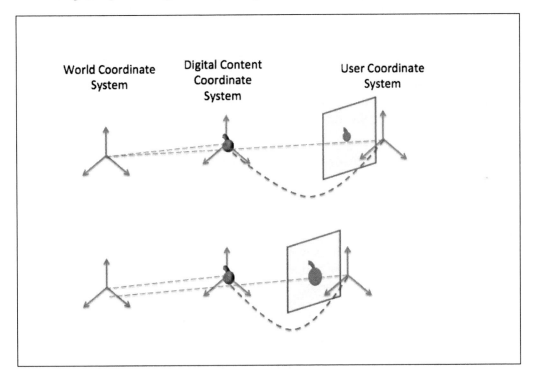

A small issue we have with this technology is related to the coordinate system used in GPS. Using latitude and longitude coordinates (what a basic GPS delivers) is not the most adapted representation for using AR. When we do 3D graphics, we are used to a Euclidian coordinate system to position digital content; position using the Cartesian coordinate system, defined in terms of X, Y, and Z coordinates. So we need to address this problem by transforming these GPS coordinates to something more adapted.

JME and GPS – tracking the location of your device

The Google Android API offers access to GPS through the Location Manager service. The Location Manager can provide you GPS data, but it can also use the network (for example, Wi-Fi and cellphone network) to pinpoint your location and give you a rough estimation of it. In Android terminology, this is named Location Provider. To use the Location Manager, you need to apply the standard Android mechanism for notifications in Android based on a listener class; LocationListener in this case.

So open the LocationAccessJME project associated with this chapter, which is a modified version of the SuperimposeJME project (*Chapter 3, Superimposing the World*).

First, we need to modify our Android manifest to allow access to the GPS sensor. They are different quality modes regarding GPS (quality of estimated location), we will authorize all of them. So add these two permissions to your AndroidManifest. xml file:

```
    <uses-permission android:name="android.permission.ACCESS_COARSE_
LOCATION"/>
    <uses-permission android:name="android.permission.ACCESS_FINE_
LOCATION"/>
```

The project has, same as before, a JME class (LocationAccessJME), an activity class (LocationAccessJMEActivity), as well as CameraPreview. What we need to do is create a LocationListener class and a LocationManager class that we add to our LocationAccessJMEActivity class:

```
    private LocationManager locationManager;
```

Inside the LocationListener class, we need to override different callback functions:

```
    private LocationListener locListener= new LocationListener() {
        ...
        @Override
```

```
public void onLocationChanged(Location location) {
    Log.d(TAG, "onLocation: " + location.toString());
    if ((com.ar4android.LocationAccessJME) app != null) {
        ((com.ar4android.LocationAccessJME) app)
            .setUserLocation(xyzposition);
    }
}
...
}
```

The onLocationChanged callback is the one which is the call for any changes in a user's location; the location parameter contains both the measured latitude and longitude (in degrees). To pass the converted data to our JME, we will use the same principle as before: call a method in our JME class using the location as argument. So setUserLocation will be called each time there is an update of the location of the user, and the new value will be available to the JME class.

Next, we need to access the location manager service and register our location listener to it, using the requestLocationUpdates function:

```
public void onResume() {
    super.onResume();
    ...
    locationManager =
    (LocationManager)getSystemService(LOCATION_SERVICE);
    locationManager.requestLocationUpdates
    (LocationManager.GPS_PROVIDER, 500, 0, locListener);
}
```

The parameters of requestLocationUpdates are the types of provider we want to use (GPS versus network), update frequency (in milliseconds), and change of position threshold (in meters) as our listener.

On the JME side, we need to define two new variables to our LocationAccessJME class:

```
//the User position which serves as intermediate storage place
  for the Android
//Location listener position update
private Vector3f mUserPosition;

//A flag indicating if a new Location is available
private boolean mNewUserPositionAvailable =false;
```

We also need to define our `setUserLocation` function, which is called from the callback in `LocationListener`:

```
public void setUserLocation(Vector3f location) {
if (!mSceneInitialized) {
  return;
}
WSG84toECEF(location,mUserPosition);
//update your POI location in reference to the user position
....
mNewUserPositionAvailable =true;
}
```

Inside this function we need to transform the position of the camera from latitude/longitude format to a Cartesian coordinate system. There are different techniques to do so; we will use the conversion algorithm from the SatSleuth website (http://www.satsleuth.com/GPS_ECEF_Datum_transformation.htm), converting our data to an **ECEF (Earth-Centered, Earth-Fixed)** format. Now we have `mUserPosition` available in ECEF format in our JME class. Each time a user's location will change, the `onLocationChange` method and `setUserLocation` will be called and we will get an updated value of `mUserPosition`. The question now is how we use this variable in our scenegraph and in relation with geo-referenced digital content (for example, POI)?

The method to use is to reference your content locally from your current position. For doing that, we need to use an additional coordinate system: the **ENU (East-North-Up)** coordinate system. For each data you have (for example, a certain number of POIs at 5 km radius from your position), you compute the location from your current position. Let's have a look at how we can do that on our ninja model, as shown in the following code:

```
Vector3f ECEFNinja=new Vector3f();
Vector3f ENUNinja=new Vector3f();
WSG84toECEF(locationNinja,ECEFNinja);
ECEFtoENU(location,mUserPosition,ECEFNinja,ENUNinja);
mNinjaPosition.set(ENUNinja.x,0,ENUNinja.y);
```

The position of the ninja in latitude-longitude format (`locationNinja`) is also converted to the ECEF format (`ECEFNinja`). From there, using the current GPS location (in latitude-longitude format and ECEF format, location, mUserPosition), we compute the position of the ninja in a local coordinate system (`ENUNinja`). Each time the user moves, his or her GPS position will be updated, transformed to ECEF format, and the local position of the content will be updated, which will trigger a different rendering. That's it! We have implemented GPS-based tracking. An illustration of the relation of the different coordinate systems is represented in the following figure:

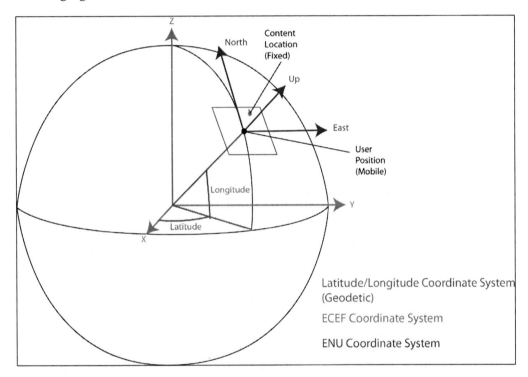

The only remaining part is to update the position of the model using the new local position. We can implement that from the `simpleUpdate` function by adding the following code:

```
if (mNewUserPositionAvailable) {
    Log.d(TAG,"update user location");
    ninja.setLocalTranslation
    (mNinjaPosition.x+0.0f,mNinjaPosition.
    y-2.5f,mNinjaPosition.z+0.0f);
    mNewUserPositionAvailable=false;
}
```

In a real AR application, you may have some 3D content positioned around your current position in a GPS coordinate system, such as having a virtual ninja positioned in Fifth street in New York, or in front of the Eiffel Tower in Paris.

Since we want to be sure, you can run this sample independently of where you are currently testing and reading the book (from New York to Timbuktu). We will modify this demo slightly for educational purposes. What we will do is add the ninja model at 10 meters from your initial GPS location (that is, first time the GPS updates), by adding the following call in setUserLocation:

```
if (firstTimeLocation) {
  //put it at 10 meters
  locationNinja.setLatitude(location.getLatitude()+0.0001);
  locationNinja.setLongitude(location.getLongitude());
  firstTimeLocation=false;
}
```

Time for testing: deploy the application on your mobile and go outside to a location where you should get a nice GPS reception (you should be able to see the sky and avoid a really cloudy day). Don't forget to activate the GPS on your device. Start the application, move around and you should see the ninja shifting positions. Congratulations, you developed your first instance of tracking for an AR application!

Knowing where you look – handling inertial sensors

With the previous example and access to GPS location, we can now update a user's location and be able to do a basic tracking in Augmented Reality. However, this tracking is only considering position of the user and not his or her orientation. If, for example, the user rotates the phone, nothing will happen, with changes being effective only if he is moving. For that we need to be able to detect changes in rotation for the user; this is where inertial sensors come in. The inertial sensors can be used to detect changes in orientation.

Understanding sensors

In the current generation of mobile phones, three types of sensors are available and useful for orientation:

- **Accelerometers**: These sensors detect the proper acceleration of your phone, also called **g-force** acceleration. Your phone is generally equipped with multi-axis model to deliver you acceleration in the 3 axes: pitch, roll, and tilt of your phone. They were the first sensors made available on mobile phones and are used for sensor-based games, being cheap to produce. With accelerometers, and a bit of elementary physics, you are able to compute the orientation of the phone. They are, however, rather inaccurate and the measured data is really noisy (which can result in getting jitters in your AR application).

- **Magnetometers**: They can detect the earth's magnetic field and act like a compass. Ideally, you can get the north direction with them by measuring the magnetic field in three dimensions and know where your phone points. The challenge with magnetometers is that they can easily be distracted by metallic objects around them, such as a watch on the user's wrist, and then indicate a wrong north direction.

- **Gyroscopes**: They measure angular velocity using the **Coriolis Effect**. The ones used in your phone are **multi-axis miniature mechanical system (MEMS)** using a vibrating mechanism. They are more accurate than the previous sensors, but their main issue is the drift: the accuracy of measurement decreases over time; after a short period your measure starts getting really inaccurate.

You can combine measurements of each of them to address their limitations, as we will see later in this chapter. Inertial sensors have been used intensively before coming to mobile phones, the most famous usage being in planes for measuring their orientation or velocity, used as an **inertial measurement unit (IMU)**. As manufacturers always try to cut down costs, quality of the sensors varies considerably between mobile devices. The effect of noise, drift, and inaccuracy will induce your AR content to jump or move without you displacing the phone or it may lead to positioning the content in the wrong orientation. Be sure you test a range of them if you want to deploy your application commercially.

Sensors in JME

Sensor access on Google Android API is made through `SensorManager`, and uses `SensorListener` to retrieve measurements. `SensorManager` doesn't give you access only to the inertial sensors, but to all the sensors present on your phone. Sensors are divided in three categories in the Android API: motion sensors, environmental sensors, and position sensors. The accelerometers and the gyroscope are defined as motion sensors; the magnetometer is defined as a position sensor. The Android API also implements some software sensors, which combine the values of these different sensors (which may include position sensor too) to provide you with motion and orientation information. The five motion sensors available are:

- `TYPE_ACCELEROMETER`
- `TYPE_GRAVITY`
- `TYPE_GYROSCOPE`
- `TYPE_LINEAR_ACCELERATION`
- `TYPE_ROTATION_VECTOR`

Please refer to the Google Developer Android website `http://developer.android.com/guide/topics/sensors/sensors_overview.html`, for more information about the characteristics of each of them. So let's open the `SensorAccessJME` project. As we did before, we define a `SensorManager` class and we will add a `Sensor` class for each of these motion sensors:

```
private SensorManager sensorManager;
Sensor rotationVectorSensor;
Sensor gyroscopeSensor;
Sensor magneticFieldSensor;
Sensor accelSensor;
Sensor linearAccelSensor;
```

We also need to define `SensorListener`, which will handle any sensor changes from the motion sensors:

```
private SensorEventListener sensorListener = new SensorEventListener()
{
    ...
@Override
public void onSensorChanged(SensorEvent event) {
  switch(event.sensor.getType()) {
      ...
      case Sensor.TYPE_ROTATION_VECTOR:
  float[] rotationVector =
  {event.values[0],event.values[1], event.values[2]};
```

```
float[] quaternion = {0.f,0.f,0.f,0.f};
sensorManager.getQuaternionFromVector
(quaternion,rotationVector);
float qw = quaternion[0]; float qx = quaternion[1];
float qy = quaternion[2];float qz = quaternion[3];
  double headingQ = Math.atan2(2*qy*qw-2*qx*qz ,
  1 - 2*qy*qy - 2*qz*qz);
double pitchQ = Math.asin(2*qx*qy + 2*qz*qw);
double rollQ = Math.atan2(2*qx*qw-2*qy*qz ,
  1 - 2*qx*qx - 2*qz*qz);
if ((com.ar4android.SensorAccessJME) app != null) {
((com.ar4android.SensorAccessJME) app).
setRotation((float)pitchQ, (float)rollQ, (float)headingQ);
}
}
}
};
```

The rotation changes could also solely be handled with Quaternions,
but we explicitly used Euler angles for a more intuitive understanding.
Privilege quaternions as composing rotations is easier and they don't
suffer from "gimbal lock".

Our listener overrides two callbacks: the onAccuracyChanged and onSensorChanged
callbacks. The onSensorChanged channel will be called for any changes in the
sensors we registered to SensorManager. Here we identify which type of sensor
changed by querying the type of event with event.sensor.getType(). For each
type of sensor, you can use the generated measurement to compute the new
orientation of the device. In this example we will only show you how to use the
value of the TYPE_ROTATION_VECTOR sensor (software sensor). The orientation
delivered by this sensor needs to be mapped to match the coordinate frame of the
virtual camera. We pass Euler angles (heading, pitch, and roll) to the JME application
to achieve this in the JME application's setRotation function (the Euler angle is just
another representation of orientation and can be calculated from Quaternions and
axis-angle representations delivered in the sensor event).

Now, having our SensorListener, we need to query SensorManager to get the
sensor service and initialize our sensors. In your onCreate method add:

```
// sensor setup
sensorManager = (SensorManager)getSystemService(SENSOR_SERVICE);
List<Sensor> deviceSensors = sensorManager.getSensorList
                              (Sensor.TYPE_ALL);
Log.d(TAG, "Integrated sensors:");
```

```
    for(int i = 0; i < deviceSensors.size(); ++i ) {
      Sensor curSensor = deviceSensors.get(i);
      Log.d(TAG, curSensor.getName() + "\t" + curSensor.getType()
      + "\t" + curSensor.getMinDelay() / 1000.0f);
    }
  initSensors();
```

After getting access to the sensor service, we query the list of all available sensors and display the results on our logcat. For initializing the sensors, we call our initSensors method, and define it as:

```
protected void initSensors(){
   //look specifically for the gyroscope first and then for the
   rotation_vector_sensor (underlying sensors vary from platform
   to platform)
gyroscopeSensor = initSingleSensor(Sensor.TYPE_GYROSCOPE,
"TYPE_GYROSCOPE");
rotationVectorSensor =
initSingleSensor(Sensor.TYPE_ROTATION_VECTOR,
"TYPE_ROTATION_VECTOR");
accelSensor = initSingleSensor(Sensor.TYPE_ACCELEROMETER,
"TYPE_ACCELEROMETER");
   linearAccelSensor =
   initSingleSensor(Sensor.TYPE_LINEAR_ACCELERATION,
   "TYPE_LINEAR_ACCELERATION");
magneticFieldSensor =
initSingleSensor(Sensor.TYPE_MAGNETIC_FIELD,
"TYPE_MAGNETIC_FIELD");
}
```

The function initSingleSensor will create an instance of Sensor and register our previously created listener with a specific type of sensor passed in argument:

```
protected Sensor initSingleSensor( int type, String name ){
Sensor newSensor = sensorManager.getDefaultSensor(type);
if(newSensor != null){
   if(sensorManager.registerListener(sensorListener, newSensor,
   SensorManager.SENSOR_DELAY_GAME)) {
     Log.i(TAG, name + " successfully registered default");
   } else {
     Log.e(TAG, name + " not registered default");
   }
} ...
return newSensor;
}
```

We shouldn't forget to unregister the listener when we quit the application, so modify your `onStop` method as follows:

```
public void onStop() {
  super.onStop();
  sensorManager.unregisterListener(sensorListener);
}
```

So, we are now set in our `Activity`. In our `SensorAccessJME` class we add following variables:

```
private Quaternion mRotXYZQ;
private Quaternion mInitialCamRotation;
private Quaternion mCurrentCamRotation;
```

The variable `mInitialCamRotation` holds the initial camera orientation, `mRotXYZQ` holds the sensor orientation mapped to the camera coordinate system, and `mCurrentCamRotation` stores the final camera rotation which is composed from multiplying `mInitialCamRotation` with `mRotXYZQ`. The `setRotation` function takes the sensor values from the Android activity and maps them to the camera coordinate system. Finally, it multiplies the current rotation values with the initial camera orientation:

```
public void setRotation(float pitch, float roll, float heading)
{
  if (!mSceneInitialized) {
    return;
  }
  mRotXYZQ.fromAngles(pitch , roll - FastMath.HALF_PI, 0);
  mCurrentCamRotation = mInitialCamRotation.mult(mRotXYZQ);
  mNewCamRotationAvailable = true;
```

As a last step, we need to use this rotation value for our virtual camera, the same as we did for our GPS example. In `simpleUpdate` you now add:

```
if (mNewCamRotationAvailable) {
  fgCam.setAxes(mCurrentCamRotation);
  mNewCamRotationAvailable = false;
}
```

So, we are now ready to run the application. It's important to consider that the natural orientation of the device, which defines the coordinate system for motion sensors, is not the same for all devices. If your device is, by default, in the portrait mode and you change it to landscape mode , the coordinate system will be rotated. In our examples we explicitly set the device orientation to landscape. Deploy your application on your device using this default orientation mode. You may need to rotate your device around to see the ninja moving on your screen, as shown in the following screenshots:

Improving orientation tracking – handling sensor fusion

One of the limitations with sensor-based tracking is the sensors. As we introduced before, some of the sensors are inaccurate, noisy, or have drift. A technique to compensate their individual issue is to combine their values to improve the overall rotation you can get with them. This technique is called sensor fusion. There are different methods for fusing the sensors, we will use the method presented by *Paul Lawitzki* with a source code under MIT License available at http://www.thousand-thoughts.com/2012/03/android-sensor-fusion-tutorial/. In this section, we will briefly explain how the technique works and how to integrate sensor fusion to our JME AR application.

Sensor fusion in a nutshell

The fusion algorithm proposed by *Paul Lawitzki* merges accelerometers, magnetometers, and gyroscope sensor data. Similar to what is done with software sensor of an Android API, accelerometers and magnetometers are first merged to get an absolute orientation (magnetometer, acting as a compass, gives you the true north). To compensate for the noise and inaccuracy of both of them, the gyroscope is used. The gyroscope, being precise but drifting over time, is used at high frequency in the system; the accelerometers and magnetometers are considered over longer periods. Here is an overview of the algorithm:

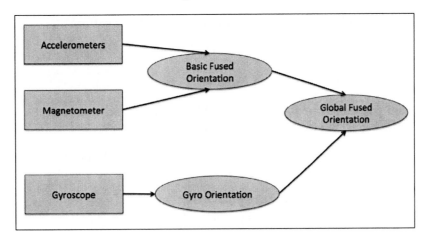

You can find more information about the details of the algorithm (complimentary filter) on *Paul Lawitzki's* webpage.

Sensor fusion in JME

Open the `SensorFusionJME` project. The sensor fusion uses a certain number of internal variables that you declare at the beginning of `SensorFusionJMEActivity`:

```
// angular speeds from gyro
private float[] gyro = new float[3]; ...
```

Also add the code of different subroutines used by the algorithm:

- `calculateAccMagOrientation`: Calculates the orientation angles from the accelerometer and magnetometer measurement
- `getRotationVectorFromGyro`: Calculates a rotation vector from the gyroscope angular speed measurement
- `gyroFunction`: Writes the gyroscope-based orientation into `gyroOrientation`
- **Two matrix transformation functions**: `getRotationMatrixFromOrientation` and `matrixMultiplication`

The main part of the processing is done in the `calculatedFusedOrientationTask` function. This function generates new fused orientation as part of `TimerTask`, a task that can be scheduled at a specific time. At the end of this function, we will pass the generated data to our JME class:

```
if ((com.ar4android.SensorFusionJME) app != null) {
    ((com.ar4android.SensorFusionJME)
    app).setRotationFused((float)(fusedOrientation[2]),
    (float)(-fusedOrientation[0]),
    (float)(fusedOrientation[1]));
    }
}
```

The argument passed to our JME activity bridge function (`setRotationFused`) is the fused orientation defined in the Euler angles format.

We also need to modify our `onSensorChanged` callback to call the subroutines used by `calculatedFusedOrientationTask`:

```
public void onSensorChanged(SensorEvent event) {
  switch(event.sensor.getType()) {
  case Sensor.TYPE_ACCELEROMETER:
    System.arraycopy(event.values, 0, accel, 0, 3);
    calculateAccMagOrientation();
```

```
      break;
  case Sensor.TYPE_MAGNETIC_FIELD:
    System.arraycopy(event.values, 0, magnet, 0, 3);
    break;
  case Sensor.TYPE_GYROSCOPE:
    gyroFunction(event)
    break;
}
```

For our activity class, the last change is to specify a task for our timer, specify the schedule rate, and the delay before the first execution. We add that to our onCreate method after the call to initSensors:

```
fuseTimer.scheduleAtFixedRate(new calculateFusedOrientationTask(),
1000, TIME_CONSTANT);
```

On the JME side, we define a new bridge function for updating the rotation (and again converting the sensor orientation into an appropriate orientation of the virtual camera):

```
public void setRotationFused(float pitch, float roll, float heading) {
  if (!mSceneInitialized) {
    return;
  } // pitch: cams x axis roll: cams y axisheading: cams z axis
  mRotXYZQ.fromAngles(pitch + FastMath.HALF_PI , roll -
  FastMath.HALF_PI, 0);
  mCurrentCamRotationFused = mInitialCamRotation.mult(mRotXYZQ);
  mNewUserRotationFusedAvailable = true;
}
```

We finally use this function in the same way as for setRotation in simpleUpdate, updating camera orientation with fgCam.setAxes(mCurrentCamRotationFused). You can now deploy the application and see the results on your device.

If you combine the LocationAccessJME and SensorAccessJME examples, you will now get full 6 degrees of freedom (6DOF) tracking, which is the foundation for a classical sensor-based AR application.

Getting content for your AR browser – the Google Places API

After knowing how to obtain your GPS position and the orientation of the phone, you are now ready to integrate great content into the live view of the camera. Would it not be cool to physically explore points of interests, such as landmarks and shops around you? We will now show you how to integrate popular location-based services such as the Google Places API to achieve exactly this. For a successful integration into your application, you will need to perform the following steps:

- Query for point of interests (POIs) around your current location
- Parse the results and extract information belonging to the POIs
- Visualize the information in your AR view

Before we start, you have to make sure that you have a valid API key for your application. For that you also need a Google account. You can obtain it by logging in with your Google account under `https://code.google.com/apis/console`.

For testing your application you can either use the default project `API Project` or create a new one. To create a new API key you need to:

1. Click on the link **Services** in the menu on the left-hand side.
2. Activate the Places API status switch.
3. Access your key by clicking on the **API access** menu entry on the left-hand side menu and looking at the **Simple API Access** area.

You can store the key in the `String mPlacesKey = "<YOUR API KEY HERE>"` variable in the `LocationAccessJME` project.

Next, we will show you how to query for POIs around the devices location, and getting some basic information such as their name and position. The integration of this information into the AR view follows the same principles as described in the *JME and GPS – tracking the location of your device* section.

Querying for POIs around your current location

Previously in this chapter, you learned how to obtain your current location in the world (latitude and longitude). You can now use this information to obtain the location of POIs around you. The Google Places API allows you to query for landmarks and businesses in the vicinity of the user via HTTP requests and returns the results as JSON or XML strings. All queries will be addressed towards URLs starting with `https://maps.googleapis.com/maps/api/place/`.

While you could easily make the queries in your web browser, you would want to have both the request sent and the response processed inside your Android application. As calling a URL and waiting for the response can take up several seconds, you would want to implement this request-response processing in a way that does not block the execution of your main program. Here we show you how to do that with threads.

In your `LocationAccessJME` project, you define some new member variables, which take care of the interaction with the Google Places API. Specifically, you create a `HttpClient` for sending your request and a list `List<POI> mPOIs`, for storing the most important information about POIs. The `POI` class is a simple helper class to store the Google Places reference string (a unique identifier in the Google Places database, the POI name, its latitude, and longitude):

```
private class POI {
   public String placesReference;
   public String name;
   public Location location;
...
}
```

Of course, you can easily extend this class to hold additional information such as street address or image URLs. To query for POIs you make a call to the `sendPlacesQuery` function. We do the call at program startup, but you can easily do it in regular intervals (for example, when the user moves a certain distance) or explicitly on a button click.

```
public void sendPlacesQuery(final Location location,  final Handler
guiHandler) throws Exception  {
Thread t = new Thread() {
public void run() {
  Looper.prepare();
  BufferedReader in = null;
  try {
    String url =
    "https://maps.googleapis.com/maps/api/place/nearbysearch/json?
    location=" + location.getLatitude() + "," +
    location.getLongitude() + "&radius=" +  mPlacesRadius +
    "&sensor=true&key=" + mPlacesKey;
    HttpConnectionParams.setConnectionTimeout
    (mHttpClient.getParams(), 10000);
    HttpResponse response;
    HttpGet get = new HttpGet(url);
    response = mHttpClient.execute(get);
```

```
Message toGUI = guiHandler.obtainMessage();
...
guiHandler.sendMessage(toGUI);
...
```

In this method, we create a new thread for each query to the Google Places service. This is very important for not blocking the execution of the main program. The response of the Places API should be a JSON string, which we pass to a `Handler` instance in the main thread to parse the JSON results, which we will discuss next.

Parsing the Google Places APIs results

Google Places returns its result in the lightweight JSON format (with XML being another option). You can use the `org.json` library delivered as a standard Android package to conveniently parse those results.

A typical JSON result for your query will look like:

```
{
    ...
    "results" : [
        {
            "geometry" : {
                "location" : {
                    "lat" : 47.07010720,
                    "lng" : 15.45455070
                },
        ...
            },
            "name" : "Sankt Leonhard",
            "reference" :
            "CpQBiQAAADXt6JM47sunYZ8vZvt0GViZDLICZi2JLRdfhHGbtK-
            ekFMjkaceN6GmECaynOnR69buuDZ6t-PKow-
            J9812tFyg3T50P0Fr39DRV3YQMpqW6YGhu5sAzArNzipS2
            tUY0ocoMNHoNSGPbuuYIDX5QURVgncFQ5K8eQL8OkPST78
            A_1KTN7icaKQV7HvvHkEQJBIQrx2r8IxIYuaVhL1mOZOsK
            BoUQj1suuhqa1k7OCtxThYqVgfGUGw",
            ...
        },
    ...
    }
```

In `handleMessage` of our handler `placesPOIQueryHandler`, we will parse this JSON string into a list of POIs, which then can be visualized in your AR view:

```
public void handleMessage(Message msg) {
  try {
    JSONObject response = new JSONObject(msg.obj.toString());
    JSONArray results = response.getJSONArray("results");
    for(int i = 0; i < results.length(); ++i) {
      JSONObject curResult = results.getJSONObject(i);
      String poiName = curResult.getString("name");
      String poiReference = curResult.getString("reference");
      double lat =
      curResult.getJSONObject("geometry").
      getJSONObject("location").getDouble("lat");
      double lng =
      curResult.getJSONObject("geometry").
      getJSONObject("location").getDouble("lng");
      Location refLoc = new
      Location(LocationManager.GPS_PROVIDER);
      refLoc.setLatitude(lat);
      refLoc.setLongitude(lng);
      mPOIs.add(new POI(poiReference, poiName, refLoc));
      ...
    }
    ...
  }
}
```

So that is it. You now have your basic POI information and with the latitude, longitude information you can easily instantiate new 3D objects in JME and position them correctly relative to your camera position, just as you did with the ninja. You can also query for more details about the POIs or filter them by various criteria. For more information on the Google Places API please visit `https://developers.google.com/places/documentation/`.

 If you want to include text in the 3D scene, we recommend avoiding the use of 3D text objects as they result in a high number of additional polygons to render. Use bitmap text instead, which you render as a texture on a mesh that can be generated.

Summary

In this chapter we introduced you to the first popular methods of mobile AR: GPS and sensor-based Augmented Reality. We introduced the basic building blocks of tracking the device location in a global reference frame, dynamically determining the device orientation, improving the robustness of orientation tracking, and finally using the popular Google Places API to retrieve information about POIs around the user which can then be integrated into the AR view.

In the next chapter we will introduce you to the second popular way of realizing mobile AR: computer vision-based Augmented Reality.

5
Same as Hollywood – Virtual on Physical Objects

In the previous chapter you learned about the basic building blocks for implementing GPS and sensor-based AR applications. If you tried the different examples we presented, you might have noticed that the feeling of getting digital objects in real space (*registration*) works but can become coarse and unstable. This is mainly due to the accuracy problems of the used sensors (GPS, accelerometer, and so on) found in smartphones or tablet devices, and the characteristics of these technologies (for example, gyroscope drifting, GPS reliance on satellite visibility, and other such technologies). In this chapter, we will introduce you to a more robust solution, with it being the second major approach for supporting mobile AR: **Computer vision-based AR**.

Computer vision-based AR doesn't rely on any external sensors but uses the content of the camera image to support tracking, which is analysis through a flow of different algorithms. With computer vision-based AR, you get a better registration between the digital and physical worlds albeit at a little higher cost in terms of processing.

Probably, without even knowing it, you have already seen computer vision-based registration. If you go to see a blockbuster action movie with lots of cinematic effects, you will sometimes notice that some digital content has been overlaid over the physical recording set (for example, fake explosions, fake background, and fake characters running). In the same way as AR, the movie industry has to deal with the registration between digital and physical content, relying on analyzing the recorded image to recover tracking and camera information (using, for example, the match matchmoving technique). However, compared to Augmented Reality, it's done offline, and not in real time, generally relying on heavy workstations for registration and visual integration.

In this chapter, we will introduce you to the different types of computer vision-based tracking for AR. We will also describe to you the integration of a well-used and high-quality tracking library for mobile AR, **Vuforia**™ by Qualcomm® Inc. With this library, we will be able to implement our first computer vision-based AR application.

Introduction to computer vision-based tracking and Vuforia™

So far, you have used the camera of the mobile phone exclusively for rendering the view of the real world as the background for your models. Computer vision-based AR goes a step further and processes each image frame to look for familiar *patterns* (or image features) in the camera image.

In a typical computer vision-based AR application, planar objects such as *frame markers* or *natural feature tracking targets* are used to position the camera in a *local coordinate system* (see *Chapter 3, Superimposing the World, Figure showing the three most common coordinate systems*). This is in contrast to the global coordinate system (the earth) used in sensor-based AR but allows for more precise and stable overlay of virtual content in this local coordinate frame. Similar to before, obtaining the tracking information allows the updating of information about the virtual camera in our 3D graphics rendering engine and automatically provides us with registration.

Choosing physical objects

In order to successfully implement computer vision-based AR, you need to understand which physical objects you can use to track the camera. Currently there are two major approaches to do this: Frame markers (**Fiducials**) and natural feature tracking targets (planar textured objects), as shown in the following figure. We will discuss both of them in the following section.

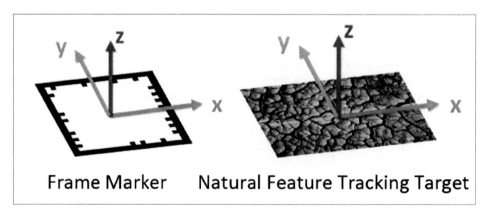

Frame Marker   Natural Feature Tracking Target

Understanding frame markers

In the early days of mobile Augmented Reality, it was of paramount importance to use computationally efficient algorithms. Computer vision algorithms are traditionally demanding as they generally rely on image analysis, complex geometric algorithms, and mathematical transformation, summing to a large number of operations that should take place at every time frame (to keep a constant frame rate at 30 Hz, you only have 33 ms for all that). Therefore, one of the first approaches to computer vision-based AR was to use relatively simple types of objects, which could be detected with computationally low-demanding algorithms, such as Fiducial markers. These markers are generally only defined at a grayscale level, simplifying their analysis and recognition in a traditional physical world (think about QR code but in 3D).

A typical algorithmic workflow for detecting these kinds of markers is depicted in the following figure and will be briefly explained next:

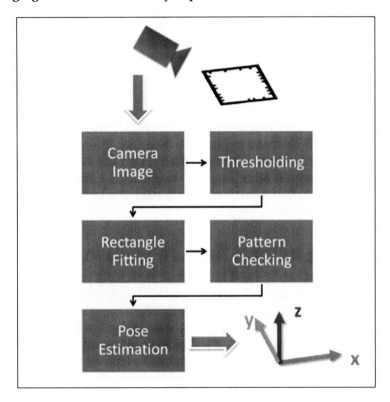

After an acquired camera image being converted to a grayscale image, the **threshold** is applied, that is, the grayscale level gets converted to a purely black and white image. The next step, **rectangle detection**, searches for edges in this simplified image, which is then followed by a process of detecting closed-contour, and potentially parallelogram shapes. Further steps are taken to ensure that the detected contour is really a parallelogram (that is, it has exactly four points and a couple of parallel lines). Once the shape is confirmed, the content of the marker is analyzed. A (binary) pattern within the border of the marker is extracted in the **pattern checking** step to *identify* the marker. This is important to be able to overlay different virtual content on different markers. For frame markers a simple bit code is used that supports 512 different combinations (and hence markers).

In the last step, the pose (that is the translation and rotation of the camera in the local coordinate system of the marker or reversely) is computed in the **pose estimation** step.

Pose computation, in its simplest form a *homography* (a mapping between points on two planes), can be used together with the intrinsic parameters to recover the translation and rotation of the camera.

In practice, this is not a one-time computation, but rather, an iterative process in which the initial pose gets refined several times to obtain more accurate results. In order to reliably estimate the camera pose, the length of at least one side (the width or height) of the marker has to be known to the system; this is typically done through a configuration step when a marker description is loaded. Otherwise, the system could not tell reliably whether a small marker is near or a large marker is far away (due to the effects of perspective projection).

Understanding natural feature tracking targets

While the frame markers can be used to efficiently track the camera pose for many applications, you will want less obtrusive objects to track. You can achieve this by employing more advanced, but also computationally expensive, algorithms. The general idea of natural feature tracking is to use a number (in theory only three, and in practice several dozens or hundreds) of local points on a target to compute the camera pose. The challenge is that these points have to be reliable, robustly detected, and tracked. This is achieved with advanced computer vision algorithms to detect and describe the local neighborhood of an **interest point** (or feature point). Interest points have sharp, crisp details (such as corners), for example, using gradient orientations, which are suitable for feature points indicated by yellow crosses in the following figure. A circle or a straight line does not have sharp features and is not suitable for interest points:

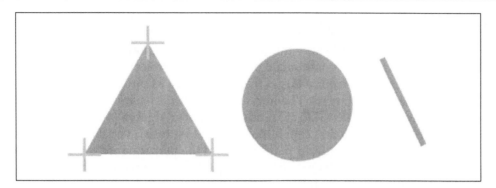

Many feature points can be found on well-textured images (such as the image of the street used throughout this chapter):

Beware that feature points cannot be well identified on images with homogenous color regions or soft edges (such as a blue sky or some computer graphics-rendered pictures).

Vuforia™ architecture

Vuforia™ is an Augmented Reality library distributed by Qualcomm® Inc. The library is free for use in non-commercial or commercial projects. The library supports frame marker and natural feature target tracking as well as multi-target, which are combinations of multiple targets. The library also features basic rendering functions (video background and OpenGL® 3D rendering), linear algebra (matrix/vector transformation), and interaction capabilities (virtual buttons). The library is actually available on both iOS and Android platforms, and the performance is improved on mobile devices equipped with Qualcomm® chipsets. An overview of the library architecture is presented in the following figure:

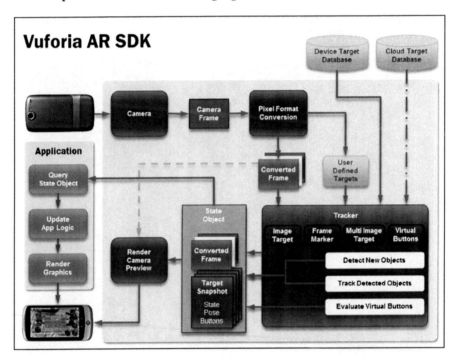

The architecture, from a client viewpoint (application box on the left of the preceding figure), offers a state object to the developer, which contains information about recognized targets as well as the camera content. We won't get into too much of details here as a list of samples is available on their website, along with full documentation and an active forum, at `http://developer.vuforia.com/`. What you need to know is that the library uses the **Android NDK** for its integration as it's being developed in C++.

This is mainly due to the gains of high-performance computation for image analysis or computer vision with C++ rather than doing it in Java (concurrent technologies also use the same approach). It's a drawback for us (as we are using JME and Java only) but a gain for you in terms of getting performances in your application.

To use the library, you generally need to follow these three steps:

- Train and create your target or markers
- Integrate the library in your application
- Deploy your application

In the next section, we will introduce you to creating and training your targets.

Configuring Vuforia™ to recognize objects

To use the Vuforia™ toolkit with natural feature tracking targets, first you need to create them. In the recent version of the library (2.0), you can automatically create your target when the application is running (online) or predefine them before deploying your application (offline). We will show you how to proceed for offline creation. First go to the Vuforia™ developer website https://developer.vuforia.com.

The first thing you need to do is to log in to the website to access the tool for creating your target. Click on the upper-right corner and register if you have not done it before. After login, you can click on **Target Manager**, the training program to create targets. The target manager is organized in a database (which can correspond to your project), and for database, you can create a list of targets, as shown in the following screenshot:

So let's create our first database. Click on **Create Database,** and enter `VuforiaJME`. Your database should appear in your **Device Databases** list. Select it to get onto the following page:

Click on **Add New Target** to create the first target. A dialog box will appear with different text fields to complete, as shown in the following screenshot:

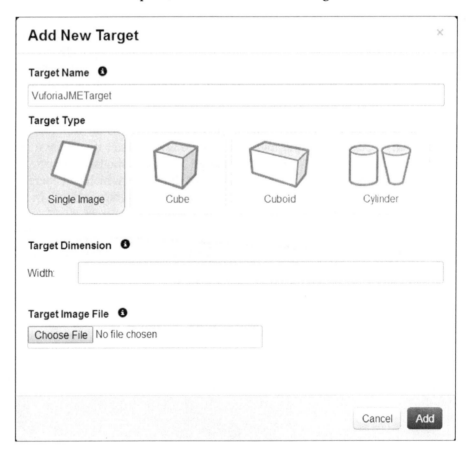

First you need to pick up a name for your target; in our case, we will call it VuforiaJMETarget. Vuforia™ allows you to create different types of targets as follows:

- **Single Image**: You create only one planar surface and use only one image. The target is generally used for printing on a page, part of a magazine, and so on.

- **Cube**: You define multiple surfaces (with multiple pictures), which will be used to track a 3D cube. This can be used for games, packaging, and so on.

- **Cuboid**: It's a variation of the cube type, as a parallelepiped with non-square faces.

Select **Single Image** target type. The target dimension defines a relative scale for your marker. The unit is not defined as it corresponds to the size of your virtual object. A good tip is to consider that everything is in centimeters or millimeters, which is generally the size of your physical marker (for example, print on an A4 or letter page). In our case, we enter the dimension in centimeters. Finally, you need to select an image which will be used for the target. As an example, you can select the stones.jpg image, which is available with the Vuforia™ sample distribution (Media directory in the *ImageTargets* example on the Vuforia™ website). To validate your configuration, click on **Add**, and wait as the image is being processed. When the processing is over, you should get a screen like the following:

The stars notify you of the quality of the target for tracking. This example has five stars, which means it will work really well. You can get more information on the Vuforia™ website on how to create a good image for a target: `https://developer.` `vuforia.com/resources/dev-guide/natural-features-and-rating`.

Our last step is now to export the created target. So select the target (tick the box next to **VuforiaJMETarget**), and click on **Download Selected Targets**. On the dialog box that appears, choose **SDK** for export and **VuforiaJME** for our database name, and save.

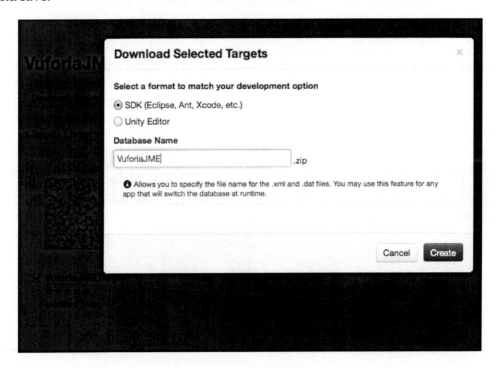

Unzip your compressed file. You will see two files: a `.dat` file and a `.xml` file. Both files are used for operating the Vuforia™ tracking at runtime. The `.dat` file specifies the feature points from your image and the `.xml` file is a configuration file. Sometimes you may want to change the size of your marker or do some basic editing without having to restart or do the training; you can modify it directly on your XML file. So now we are ready with our target for implementing our first Vuforia™ project!

Putting it together – Vuforia™ with JME

In this section we will show you how to integrate Vuforia™ with JME. We will use a natural feature-tracking target for this purpose. So open the **VuforiaJME** project in your Eclipse to start. As you can already observe, there are two main changes compared to our previous projects:

- The camera preview class is gone
- There is a new directory in the project root named `jni`

The first change is due to the way Vuforia™ manages the camera. Vuforia™ uses its own camera handle and camera preview integrated in the library. Therefore, we'll need to query the video image through the Vuforia™ library to display it on our scene graph (using the same principle as seen in *Chapter 2, Viewing the World*).

The `jni` folder contains C++ source code, which is required for Vuforia™. To integrate Vuforia™ with JME, we need to interoperate Vuforia's low-level part (C++) with the high-level part (Java). It means we will need to compile C++ and Java code and transfer data between them. If you have done it, you'll need to download and install the Android NDK before going further (as explained in *Chapter 1, Augmented Reality Concepts and Tools*).

The C++ integration

The C++ layer is based on a modified version of the **ImageTargets** example available on the Vuforia™ website. The `jni` folder contains the following files:

- `MathUtils.cpp` and `MathUtils.h`: Utilities functions for mathematical computation
- `VuforiaNative.cpp`: This is the main C++ class that interacts with our Java layer
- `Android.mk` and `Application.mk`: These contains configuration files for compilation

Open the `Android.mk` file, and check if the path to your Vuforia™ installation is correct in the `QCAR_DIR` directory. Use only a relative path to make it cross-platform (on MacOS with the android ndk r9 or higher, an absolute path will be concatenated with the current directory and result in an incorrect directory path).

Now open the `VuforiNative.cpp` file. A lot of functions are defined in the files but only three are relevant to us:

- `Java_com_ar4android_VuforiaJMEActivity_loadTrackerData(JNIEnv *, jobject)`: This is the function for loading our specific target (created in the previous section)

- `virtual void QCAR_onUpdate(QCAR::State& state)`: This is the function to query the camera image and transfer it to the Java layer

- `Java_com_ar4android_VuforiaJME_updateTracking(JNIEnv *env, jobject obj)`: This function is used to query the position of the targets and transfer it to the Java layer

The first step will be to use our specific target in our application and the first function. So copy and paste the `VuforiaJME.dat` and `VuforiaJME.xml` files to your assets directory (there should already be two target configurations). Vuforia™ configures the target that will be used based on the XMLconfiguration file. `loadTrackerData` gets first access to `TrackerManager` and `imageTracker` (which is a tracker for non-natural features):

```
JNIEXPORT int JNICALL
Java_com_ar4android_VuforiaJMEActivity_loadTrackerData(JNIEnv *,
jobject)
{
    LOG("Java_com_ar4android_VuforiaJMEActivity_ImageTargets_
      loadTrackerData");

    // Get the image tracker:
    QCAR::TrackerManager& trackerManager = QCAR::TrackerManager::
                                    getInstance();
    QCAR::ImageTracker* imageTracker = static_
      cast<QCAR::ImageTracker*>(trackerManager.
      getTracker(QCAR::Tracker::IMAGE_TRACKER));
    if (imageTracker == NULL)
    {
        LOG("Failed to load tracking data set because the
          ImageTracker has not been initialized.");
        return 0;
    }
}
```

The next step is to create a specific target, such as instancing a dataset. In this example, one dataset is created, named `dataSetStonesAndChips`:

```
// Create the data sets:
dataSetStonesAndChips = imageTracker->createDataSet();
```

```
if (dataSetStonesAndChips == 0)
{
    LOG("Failed to create a new tracking data.");
    return 0;
}
```

After we load the configuration of the targets in the created instance, this is where we set up our VuforiaJME target:

```
// Load the data sets:
if (!dataSetStonesAndChips->load("VuforiaJME.xml",
  QCAR::DataSet::STORAGE_APPRESOURCE))
{
    LOG("Failed to load data set.");
    return 0;
}
```

Finally we can activate the dataset by calling the `activateDataSet` function. If you don't activate the dataset, the target will be loaded and initialized in the tracker but won't be tracked until activation:

```
// Activate the data set:
if (!imageTracker->activateDataSet(dataSetStonesAndChips))
{
    LOG("Failed to activate data set.");
    return 0;
}

LOG("Successfully loaded and activated data set.");
return 1;
}
```

Once we have our target initialized, we need to get the real view of the world with Vuforia™. The concept is the same as we have seen before: using a video background camera in the JME class and updating it with an image. However, here, the image is not coming from a Java `Camera.PreviewCallback` but from Vuforia™. In Vuforia™ the best place to get the video image is in the `QCAR_onUpdate` function. This function is called just after the tracker gets updated. An image can be retrieved by querying a frame on the State object of Vuforia™ with `getFrame()`. A frame can contain multiple images, as the camera image is in different formats (for example, YUV, RGB888, GREYSCALE, RGB565, and so on). In the previous example, we used the RGB565 format in our JME class. We will do the same here. So our class will start as:

```
class ImageTargets_UpdateCallback : public QCAR::UpdateCallback
{
    virtual void QCAR_onUpdate(QCAR::State& state)
    {
```

```
//inspired from:
//https://developer.vuforia.com/forum/faq/android-how-can-i-
    access-camera-image

QCAR::Image *imageRGB565 = NULL;
    QCAR::Frame frame = state.getFrame();
`for (int i = 0; i < frame.getNumImages(); ++i) {
        const QCAR::Image *image = frame.getImage(i);
        if (image->getFormat() == QCAR::RGB565) {
            imageRGB565 = (QCAR::Image*)image;

            break;
        }
    }
```

The function parses a list of images in the frame and retrieves the RGB565 image.
Once we get this image, we need to transfer it to the **Java Layer**. For doing that you
can use a JNI function:

```
if (imageRGB565) {
    JNIEnv* env = 0;

    if ((javaVM != 0) && (activityObj != 0) && (javaVM-
        >GetEnv((void**)&env, JNI_VERSION_1_4) == JNI_OK)) {

        const short* pixels = (const short*) imageRGB565-
            >getPixels();
        int width = imageRGB565->getWidth();
        int height = imageRGB565->getHeight();
        int numPixels = width * height;

        jbyteArray pixelArray = env->NewByteArray
            (numPixels * 2);
        env->SetByteArrayRegion(pixelArray, 0, numPixels * 2,
            (const jbyte*) pixels);
        jclass javaClass = env->GetObjectClass(activityObj);
        jmethodID method = env-> GetMethodID(javaClass,
            "setRGB565CameraImage", "([BII)V");
        env->CallVoidMethod(activityObj, method, pixelArray,
            width, height);

        env->DeleteLocalRef(pixelArray);

    }
}

};
```

In this example, we get information about the size of the image and a pointer on the raw data of the image. We use a JNI function named `setRGB565CameraImage`, which is defined in our `Java Activity` class. We call this function from C++ and pass in argument the content of the image (`pixelArray`) as `width` and `height` of the image. So each time the tracker updates, we retrieve a new camera image and send it to the Java layer by calling the `setRGB565CameraImage` function. The JNI mechanism is really useful and you can use it for passing any data, from a sophisticated computation process back to your Java class (for example, physics, numerical simulation, and so on).

The next step is to retrieve the location of the targets from the tracking. We will do that from the `updateTracking` function. As before, we get an instance of the State object from Vuforia™. The State object contains `TrackableResults`, which is a list of the identified targets in the video image (identified here as being recognized as a target and their position identified):

```
JNIEXPORT void JNICALL
Java_com_ar4android_VuforiaJME_updateTracking(JNIEnv *env,
  jobject obj)
{
    //LOG("Java_com_ar4android_VuforiaJMEActivity_GLRenderer_
      renderFrame");

    //Get the state from QCAR and mark the beginning of a rendering
      section
    QCAR::State state = QCAR::Renderer::getInstance().begin();

    // Did we find any trackables this frame?
    for(int tIdx = 0; tIdx < state.getNumTrackableResults(); tIdx++)
    {
        // Get the trackable:
        const QCAR::TrackableResult* result = state.
          getTrackableResult(tIdx);
```

In our example, we have only one target activated, so if we get a result, it will obviously be our marker. We can then directly query the position information from it. If you had multiple activated markers, you will need to identify which one is which, by getting information from the result by calling `result->getTrackable()`.

The position of `trackable` is queried by calling `result->getPose()`, which returns a matrix defining a linear transformation. This transformation gives you the position of the marker relative to the camera position. Vuforia™ uses a computer-vision coordinate system (x on the left, y down, and z away from you), which is different from JME, so we will have to do some conversion later on. For now, what we will do first is inverse the transformation, to get the position of the camera relative to the marker; this will make the marker the reference coordinate system for our virtual content. So you will do some basic mathematical operations as follows:

```
QCAR::Matrix44F modelViewMatrix = QCAR::Tool::
  convertPose2GLMatrix(result->getPose());

QCAR::Matrix44F inverseMV = MathUtil::
  Matrix44FInverse(modelViewMatrix);
QCAR::Matrix44F invTranspMV = MathUtil::
  Matrix44FTranspose(inverseMV);

float cam_x = invTranspMV.data[12];
float cam_y = invTranspMV.data[13];
float cam_z = invTranspMV.data[14];

float cam_right_x = invTranspMV.data[0];
float cam_right_y = invTranspMV.data[1];
float cam_right_z = invTranspMV.data[2];
float cam_up_x = invTranspMV.data[4];
float cam_up_y = invTranspMV.data[5];
float cam_up_z = invTranspMV.data[6];
float cam_dir_x = invTranspMV.data[8];
float cam_dir_y = invTranspMV.data[9];
float cam_dir_z = invTranspMV.data[10];
```

Now we have the location (`cam_x,y,z`) as well as the orientation of our camera (`cam_right_/cam_up_/cam_dir_x,y,z`).

The last step is to transfer this information to the Java layer. We will use JNI again for this operation. What we also need is information about the internal parameters of our camera. This is similar to what was discussed in *Chapter 3, Superimposing the World*, but now it has been done here with Vuforia™. For that, you can access the `CameraCalibration` object from `CameraDevice`:

```
float nearPlane = 1.0f;
float farPlane = 1000.0f;
const QCAR::CameraCalibration& cameraCalibration = QCAR::
  CameraDevice::getInstance().getCameraCalibration();
```

```
QCAR::Matrix44F projectionMatrix = QCAR::Tool::
   getProjectionGL(cameraCalibration, nearPlane, farPlane);
```

We can easily transform the projection transformation to a more readable format for the camera configuration, such as its field of view (fovDegrees), which we also have to adapt to allow for differences in the aspect ratios of the camera sensor and the screen:

```
QCAR::Vec2F size = cameraCalibration.getSize();
QCAR::Vec2F focalLength = cameraCalibration.getFocalLength();
float fovRadians = 2 * atan(0.5f * size.data[1] /
   focalLength.data[1]);
float fovDegrees = fovRadians * 180.0f / M_PI;
float aspectRatio=(size.data[0]/size.data[1]);

float viewportDistort=1.0;
if (viewportWidth != screenWidth)        {
   viewportDistort = viewportWidth / (float) screenWidth;
      fovDegrees=fovDegrees*viewportDistort;
      aspectRatio=aspectRatio/viewportDistort;
}
if (viewportHeight != screenHeight)  {
   viewportDistort = viewportHeight / (float) screenHeight;
      fovDegrees=fovDegrees/viewportDistort;
      aspectRatio=aspectRatio*viewportDistort;
}
```

We then call three JNI functions to transfer the field of view (setCameraPerspectiveNative), camera position (setCameraPoseNative) and camera orientation (setCameraOrientationNative) to our Java layer. These three functions are time defined in the VuforiaJME class, which allows us to quickly modify our virtual camera:

```
jclass activityClass = env->GetObjectClass(obj);
        jmethodID setCameraPerspectiveMethod = env->GetMethodID
          (activityClass,"setCameraPerspectiveNative", "(FF)V");
        env->CallVoidMethod(obj,setCameraPerspectiveMethod,
          fovDegrees,aspectRatio);
        jmethodID setCameraViewportMethod = env->GetMethodID
          (activityClass,"setCameraViewportNative", "(FFFF)V");
        env->CallVoidMethod(obj,setCameraViewportMethod,viewportWidth,
          viewportHeight,cameraCalibration.getSize().
          data[0],cameraCalibration.getSize().data[1]);
```

```
    // jclass activityClass = env->GetObjectClass(obj);
    jmethodID setCameraPoseMethod = env->GetMethodID
        (activityClass,"setCameraPoseNative", "(FFF)V");
    env->CallVoidMethod(obj,setCameraPoseMethod,cam_x,cam_y,
        cam_z);

    //jclass activityClass = env->GetObjectClass(obj);
    jmethodID setCameraOrientationMethod = env->GetMethodID
        (activityClass,"setCameraOrientationNative", "(FFFFFFFFF)V");
    env->CallVoidMethod(obj,setCameraOrientationMethod,
        cam_right_x,cam_right_y,cam_right_z,
    cam_up_x,cam_up_y,cam_up_z,cam_dir_x,cam_dir_y,cam_dir_z);

}

    QCAR::Renderer::getInstance().end();
}
```

The last step will be to compile the program. So run a command shell, and go the `jni` directory containing the files. From there you need to call the `ndk-build` function. The function is defined in your `android-ndk-r9d` directory, so be sure it's accessible from your path. If everything goes well, you should see the following:

```
Install         : libQCAR.so => libs/armeabi-v7a/libQCAR.so
Compile++ arm   : VuforiaNative <= VuforiaNative.cpp
SharedLibrary   : libVuforiaNative.so
Install         : libVuforiaNative.so => libs/armeabi-v7a/
                  libVuforiaNative.so
```

Time to go back to Java!

The Java integration

The Java layer defines the function previously called using similar classes from our *Superimpose* example. The first function is the `setRGB565CameraImage` function which handles the video image as in the previous examples.

The other JNI functions will modify the characteristics of our foreground camera. Specifically, we modify the left axis of the JME camera to match the coordinate system used by Vuforia™ (as depicted in the figure in the *Choosing physical objects* section).

```
    public void setCameraPerspectiveNative(float fovY,float aspectRatio)
    {
            fgCam.setFrustumPerspective(fovY,aspectRatio, 1, 1000);
    }
```

```
public void setCameraPoseNative(float cam_x,float cam_y,float cam_z)
{
        fgCam.setLocation(new Vector3f(cam_x,cam_y,cam_z));
}

public void setCameraOrientationNative(float cam_right_x,float
  cam_right_y,float cam_right_z,
float cam_up_x,float cam_up_y,float cam_up_z,float cam_dir_x,
  float cam_dir_y,float cam_dir_z) {
    //left,up,direction
    fgCam.setAxes(new Vector3f(-cam_right_x,-cam_right_y,
      -cam_right_z),
      new Vector3f(-cam_up_x,-cam_up_y,-cam_up_z),
      new Vector3f(cam_dir_x,cam_dir_y,cam_dir_z));
}
```

Finally, we have to adjust the viewport of the background camera, which shows the camera image, to prevent 3D objects from floating above the physical target:

```
public void setCameraViewportNative(float viewport_w,float
viewport_h,float size_x,float size_y) {
    float newWidth = 1.f;
    float newHeight = 1.f;

    if (viewport_h != settings.getHeight())
    {
      newWidth=viewport_w/viewport_h;
      newHeight=1.0f;
      videoBGCam.resize((int)viewport_w,(int)viewport_h,true);
      videoBGCam.setParallelProjection(true);
    }
    float viewportPosition_x =  (((int)(settings.getWidth()   -
      viewport_w)) / (int) 2);//+0
    float viewportPosition_y =  (((int)(settings.getHeight() -
      viewport_h)) / (int) 2);//+0
    float viewportSize_x = viewport_w;//2560
    float viewportSize_y = viewport_h;//1920

    //transform in normalized coordinate
    viewportPosition_x =  (float)viewportPosition_x/(float)
      viewport_w;
    viewportPosition_y =  (float)viewportPosition_y/(float)
      viewport_h;
```

```
        viewportSize_x = viewportSize_x/viewport_w;
        viewportSize_y = viewportSize_y/viewport_h;

    //adjust for viewport start (modify video quad)
        mVideoBGGeom.setLocalTranslation(-0.5f*newWidth+
          viewportPosition_x,-0.5f*newHeight+viewportPosition_y,0.f);
    //adust for viewport size (modify video quad)
    mVideoBGGeom.setLocalScale(newWidth, newHeight, 1.f);
}
```

And that's it. What we want to outline again here is the concept behind it:

- The camera model used in your tracker is matched with your virtual camera (in this example CameraCalibration from Vuforia™ to our JME Virtual Camera). This will guarantee us a correct registration.

- You track a target in your camera coordinate system (in this example, a natural feature target from Vuforia™). This tracking replaces our GPS as seen previously, and uses a local coordinate system.

- The position of this target is used to modify the pose of your virtual camera (in this example, transferring the detected position from C++ to Java with JNI, and updating our JME Virtual Camera). As we repeat the process for each frame, we have a full 6DOF registration between physical (the target) and virtual (our JME scene).

Your results should look similar to the one in the following figure:

Summary

In this chapter, we introduced you to computer vision-based AR. We developed an application with the Vuforia™ library and showed you how to integrate it with JME. You are now ready to create natural feature tracking-based AR applications. In this demo, you can move your device around the marker and see the virtual content from every direction. In the next chapter, we will learn how we can do more in terms of interaction. How about being able to select the model and play with it?

6
Make It Interactive – Create the User Experience

Over the course of the previous chapters, we've learned the essentials of creating augmentations using the two most common AR approaches: sensor-based and computer vision-based AR. We are now able to overlay digital content over a view of the physical world, support AR tracking, and handle account registration (on a target or outdoors).

However, we can merely navigate the augmented world around them. Wouldn't it be cool to allow the users to also interact with the virtual content in an intuitive way? User interaction is a major component in the development of any application. As we are focusing here on the user interaction with 3D content (3D interaction), the following are three main categories of interaction techniques that can be developed:

- **Navigation**: Moving around a scene and selecting a specific viewpoint. In AR, this navigation is done by physical motion (such as, walking on the street or turning a table) and can be complemented with additional virtual functions (for example, map view, navigation path, freeze mode, and so on).

- **Manipulation**: Selecting, moving, and modifying objects. In AR, this can be done on physical and virtual elements, through a range of traditional methods (for example, ray picking), and novel interaction paradigms (for example, tangible user interfaces).

- **System control**: Adapting the parameters of your application, including rendering, polling processes, and application dependent content. In AR, it can correspond to adjusting tracking parameters or visualization techniques (for example, presenting the distance to your POI in an AR Browser).

In this chapter we will show you a subset of some of the commonly used AR interaction techniques. We will show you how to develop three interaction techniques, including ray picking, proximity-based interaction, and 3D motion gesture-based interaction. This is the next step in designing an AR Application and a fundamental brick in our AR layer (See *Chapter 1, Augmented Reality Concepts and Tools*).

Pick the stick – 3D selection using ray picking

3D interaction on desktop computers made use of a limited set of devices, including the keyboard, mouse, or joystick (for games). On a smartphone (or tablet), interaction is mainly driven by touch or sensor input. From an interaction input (the sensor data, such as x and y coordinates on the screen, or the event type, such as click or dwell), you can develop different interaction techniques, such as ray picking, steering navigation, and so on. For mobile AR, a large set of interaction techniques can be used for 2D or 3D interactions. In this section, we will look at using touch input combined with a technique named **ray picking**.

The concept of ray picking is to use a virtual ray going from your device to your environment (which is the target) and detect what it hits along the way. When you get a hit on some object (for example, the ray intersects with one of your virtual characters), you can consider this object picked (selected) and start to manipulate it. Here, we will only look at how we can pick an object in JME. In the sample code, you can extend the object to support further manipulation, for example, when an object is hit and picked, you can detect sliding touch motion and translate the object, make it explode, or use the hit as a shooting ray for some game, and so on.

So let's start. In JME, you can use either an Android-specific function for the input (via `AndroidInput`) or the same one you would use in a desktop application (`MouseInput`). JME on Android, by default, maps any touch event as a mouse event that allows us to have (almost) the same code working on Android and your desktop. We will choose the following solution for this project; as an exercise, you can try to use `AndroidInput` (look into `AndroidTouchInputListener` to use `AndroidInput`).

Open the `RayPickingJME` example. It's using the same base code as `VuforiaJME` and our picking method is based on a JME example, for this picking method please visit the following link: `http://jmonkeyengine.org/wiki/doku.php/jme3:beginner:hello_picking`.

The first thing to do is add the different packages necessary for ray picking in our `RayPickingJME` class:

```
import com.jme3.math.Ray;
import com.jme3.collision.CollisionResult;
import com.jme3.collision.CollisionResults;
import com.jme3.input.MouseInput;
import com.jme3.input.controls.ActionListener;
import com.jme3.input.controls.KeyTrigger;
import com.jme3.input.controls.MouseButtonTrigger;
```

To be able to pick an object, we need to declare some global variables in the scope of our `RayPicking` class:

- `Node shootables`
- `Geometry geom`

The next step is to add a listener to our class. If you've never done Android or JME programming, you may not know what a listener is. A **listener** is an event handler technique that can listen to any of the activities happening in a class and provide specific methods to handle any event. For example, if you have a mouse button click event, you can create a listener for it that has an `onPushEvent()` method where you can install your own code. In JME, event management and listeners are organized into two components, controlled by using the `InputManager` class:

- **Trigger mapping**: Using this you can associate the device input can with a trigger name, for example, clicking on the mouse can be associated with `Press` or `Shoot` or `MoveEntity`, and so on.

- **Listener**: Using this you can associate the trigger name with a specific listener; either `ActionListener` (used for discrete events, such as "button pressed") or `AnalogListener` (used for continuous events, such as the amplitude of a joystick movement).

So, in your `simpleInitApp` procedure, add the following code:

```
inputManager.addMapping("Shoot",          // Declare...
  newKeyTrigger(KeyInput.KEY_SPACE),  // trigger 1: spacebar, or
  newMouseButtonTrigger(0));          // trigger 2: left-button
    click
inputManager.addListener(actionListener, "Shoot");
```

So, here, we map the occasions when the spacebar is pressed (even when using a virtual keyboard) and mouse click (which is a touch action on our mobile) to the trigger name `Shoot`. This trigger name is associated with the `ActionListener` event listener that we've named `actionListener`. The action listener will be where we do the ray picking; so, on a touchscreen device, by touching the screen, you can activate `actionListener` (using the trigger `Shoot`).

Our next step is to define the list of objects that can potentially be hit by our ray picking. A good technique for that is to regroup them under a specific group node. In the following code, we will create a box object and place it under a group node named `shootables`:

```
Box b = new Box(7, 4, 6); // create cube shape at the origin
geom = new Geometry("Box", b);  // create cube geometry from the shape
Material mat = new Material(assetManager,
"Common/MatDefs/Misc/Unshaded.j3md");  // create a simple material
mat.setColor("Color", ColorRGBA.Red);   // set color of material to
blue
geom.setMaterial(mat);          // set the cube's material
geom.setLocalTranslation(new Vector3f(0.0f,0.0f,6.0f));

shootables = new Node("Shootables");
shootables.attachChild(geom);
rootNode.attachChild(shootables);
```

Now we have our touch mapping and our objects that can be hit. We only need to implement our listener. The way to ray cast in JME is similar to that in many other libraries; we use the hit coordinates (defined in the screen coordinates), transform them using our camera, create a ray, and run a hit. In our AR example, we will use the AR camera, which is updated by our computer vision-based tracker `fgCam`. So, the code is the same in AR as for another virtual game, except that here, our camera position is updated by the tracker.

We create a `Ray` object and run a picking test (hitting test) by calling `collideWith` for our list object that can be hit (`shootables`). Results of the collision will be stored in a `CollisionResults` object. So, our listener's code looks like the following code:

```
privateActionListeneractionListener = new ActionListener() {

public void onAction(String name, booleankeyPressed, float tpf)
  {
    Log.d(TAG,"Shooting.");
```

```
if (name.equals("Shoot") && !keyPressed) {

    // 1. Reset results list.
    CollisionResults results = new CollisionResults();

    // 2. Mode 1: user touch location.
    Vector2f click2d = inputManager.getCursorPosition();
    Vector3f click3d = fgCam.getWorldCoordinates(
    new Vector2f(click2d.x, click2d.y), 0f).clone();
    Vector3f dir = fgCam.getWorldCoordinates(
    new Vector2f(click2d.x, click2d.y),
      1f).subtractLocal(click3d).normalizeLocal();
    Ray ray = new Ray(click3d, dir);

    // 2. Mode 2: using screen center
    //Aim the ray from fgcamloc to fgcam direction.
    //Ray ray = new Ray(fgCam.getLocation(),
      fgCam.getDirection());

    // 3. Collect intersections between Ray and Shootables in
      results list.
    shootables.collideWith(ray, results);

...
```

So, what do we do with the result? As explained earlier in the book, you can manipulate it in a different way. We will do something simple here; we will detect whether or not our box is selected, and if it is, change its color to red for no intersection and green if there is an intersection. We first print the results for debugging, where you can use the getCollision() function to detect which object has been hit (getGeometry()), at what distance (getDistance()), and the point of contact (getContactPoint()):

```
for (int i = 0; i<results.size(); i++) {
  // For each hit, we know distance, impact point, name of
    geometry.
  floatdist = results.getCollision(i).getDistance();
  Vector3f pt = results.getCollision(i).getContactPoint();
  String hit = results.getCollision(i).getGeometry().getName();

  Log.d(TAG,"* Collision #" + i + hit);
  //         Log.d(TAG," You shot " + hit + " at " + pt + ", "
    + dist + "wu away.");
}
```

So, by using the preceding code we can detect whether or not we have any result, and since we only have one object in our scene, we consider that if we got a hit, it's our object, so we change the color of the object to green. If we don't get any hit, since there is only our object, we turn it red:

```
if (results.size() > 0) {
    // The closest collision point is what was truly hit:
CollisionResult closest = results.getClosestCollision();

closest.getGeometry().getMaterial().setColor("Color",
    ColorRGBA.Green);
} else {
    geom.getMaterial().setColor("Color", ColorRGBA.Red);
}
```

You should get a result similar to that shown in the following screenshot (hit: left, miss: right):

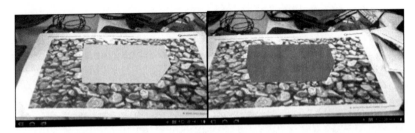

You can now deploy and run the example; touch the object on the screen and see our box changing color!

Proximity-based interaction

Another type of interaction in AR is using the relation between the camera and a physical object. If you have a target placed on a table and you move around with your device to look at a virtual object from different angles, you can also use that to create interaction. The idea is simple: you can detect any change in spatial transformation between your camera (on your moving device) and your target (placed on a table), and trigger some events. For example, you can detect if the camera is under a specific angle, if it's looking at the target from above, and so on.

In this example, we will implement a **proximity** technique that can be used to create creating some cool animation and effects. The proximity technique uses the distance between the AR camera and a computer vision-based target.

So, open the `ProximityBasedJME` project in your Eclipse. Again, this project is also based on the `VuforiaJME` example.

First, we create three objects—a box, a sphere, and a torus—using three different colors—red, green and blue—as follows:

```
Box b = new Box(7, 4, 6); // create cube shape at the origin
geom1 = new Geometry("Box", b);  // create cube geometry from
    the shape
Material mat = new Material(assetManager,
    "Common/MatDefs/Misc/Unshaded.j3md");  // create a simple
    material
mat.setColor("Color", ColorRGBA.Red);   // set color of
    material to red
geom1.setMaterial(mat);                        // set the cube's
    material


geom1.setLocalTranslation(new Vector3f(0.0f,0.0f,6.0f));


rootNode.attachChild(geom1);             // make the cube
    appear in the scene


Sphere s = new Sphere(12,12,6);
geom2 = new Geometry("Sphere", s);   // create sphere geometry
    from the shape
Material mat2 = new Material(assetManager,
    "Common/MatDefs/Misc/Unshaded.j3md");  // create a simple
    material
mat2.setColor("Color", ColorRGBA.Green);    // set color of
    material to green
geom2.setMaterial(mat2);                      // set the sphere's
    material


geom2.setLocalTranslation(new Vector3f(0.0f,0.0f,6.0f));


rootNode.attachChild(geom2);              // make the sphere
    appear in the scene


Torus= new Torus(12, 12, 2, 6); // create torus shape at
    the origin
geom3 = new Geometry("Torus", t);  // create torus geometry
    from the shape
Material mat3 = new Material(assetManager,
    "Common/MatDefs/Misc/Unshaded.j3md");  // create a simple
    material
mat3.setColor("Color", ColorRGBA.Blue);   // set color of
    material to blue
geom3.setMaterial(mat3);                   // set the
    torus material
```

```
geom3.setLocalTranslation(new Vector3f(0.0f,0.0f,6.0f));

rootNode.attachChild(geom3);                    // make the torus
   appear in the scene
```

In a large number of scene graph libraries, you will often find a switch node that allows the representation of an object based on some parameters to be switched, such as the distance from the object to the camera. JME doesn't have a switch node, so we will simulate its behavior. We will change which object is displayed (box, sphere, or torus) as a function of its distance from the camera. The simple way to do that is to add or remove objects that shouldn't be displayed at a certain distance.

To implement the proximity technique, we query the location of our AR camera (fgCam.getLocation()). From that location, you can compute the distance to some objects or just the target. The distance to the target is, by definition, similar to the distance of the location (expressed as a vector with three dimensions) of the camera. So, what we do is define three ranges for our object as follows:

- **Camera distance 50 and more**: Shows the cube
- **Camera distance 40-50**: Shows the sphere
- **Camera distance under 40**: Shows the torus

The resulting code in the simpleUpdate method is rather simple:

```
Vector3f pos=new Vector3f();

pos=fgCam.getLocation();

if (pos.length()>50.)
{
   rootNode.attachChild(geom1);
   rootNode.detachChild(geom2);
   rootNode.detachChild(geom3);

}
else
   if (pos.length()>40.)
   {
      rootNode.detachChild(geom1);
```

```
      rootNode.attachChild(geom2);
      rootNode.detachChild(geom3);
   },
   else
   {
      rootNode.detachChild(geom1);
      rootNode.detachChild(geom2);
      rootNode.attachChild(geom3);
   }
```

Run your example and change the distance of the device to that of the tracking target. This will affect the object which is presented. A cube will appear when you are far away (as shown on the left-hand side of the following figure), torus when you are close (as shown on the right-hand side of the following figure), and a sphere in between (as shown in the center of the following figure):

Simple gesture recognition using accelerometers

In *Chapter 4, Locating in the World,* you were introduced to the various sensors that are built into the typical Android device. You learned how to use them to derive the orientation of your device. However, there is much more you can do with those sensors, specifically accelerometers. If you have ever played Wii games, you were surely fascinated by the natural interaction you could achieve by waving the Wiimote around (for example, when playing a tennis or golf Wii game). Interestingly, the Wiimote uses similar accelerometers to many Android smartphones, so you can actually implement similar interaction methods as with the Wiimote. For complex 3D-motion gestures (such as drawing a figure eight in the air), you will need either some machine learning background or access to use libraries such as the one at the following link: `http://www.dfki.de/~rnessel/tools/gesture_recognition/gesture_recognition.html`. However, if you only want to recognize simple gestures, you can do that easily in a few lines of code. Next, we will show you how to recognize simple gestures such as a shake gesture, that is, quickly waving your phone back and forth several times.

If you have a look at the sample project ShakeItJME, you will notice that it is, to a large degree, identical to the SensorFusionJME project from *Chapter 4, Locating in the World*. Indeed, we only need to perform a few simple steps to extend any application that already uses accelerometers. In ShakeItJMEActivity, you first add some variables that are relevant for the shake detection, including mainly variables for storing timestamps of accelerometer events (mTimeOfLastShake, mTimeOfLastForce, and mLastTime), ones for storing past accelerometer forces (mLastAccelValX, mLastAccelValY, and mLastAccelValZ), and a number of thresholds for shake durations, timeouts (SHAKE_DURATION_THRESHOLD, TIME_BETWEEN_ACCEL_EVENTS_THRESHOLD, and SHAKE_TIMEOUT), and a minimum number of accelerometer forces and sensor samples (ACCEL_FORCE_THRESHOLD and ACCEL_EVENT_COUNT_THRESHOLD).

Next, you simply add a call to the detectShake() method in your SensorEventListener::onSensorChanged method in the Sensor.TYPE_ACCELEROMETER section of code.

The detectShake() method is at the core of your shake detection:

```
public void detectShake(SensorEvent event) {
  ...
    floatcurAccForce = Math.abs(event.values[2] - mLastAccelValZ) /
      timeDiff;
    if (curAccForce> ACCEL_FORCE_THRESHOLD) {
      mShakeCount++;
      if ((mShakeCount>= ACCEL_EVENT_COUNT_THRESHOLD) && (now -
        mTimeOfLastShake> SHAKE_DURATION_THRESHOLD)) {
        mTimeOfLastShake = now;mShakeCount = 0;
        if ((com.ar4android.ShakeItJME) app != null) {
          ((com.ar4android.ShakeItJME) app).onShake();
        }
      }
    }
  ...
  }
}
```

In this method, you basically check whether or not accelerometer values in a certain time frame are greater than the threshold value. If they are, you call the onShake() method of your JME app and integrate the event into your application logic. Note that, in this example, we only use the accelerometer values in the z direction, that is, parallel to the direction in which the camera is pointing. You can easily extend this to also include sideways shake movements by incorporating the x and y values of the accelerometer in the computation of curAccForce. As an example of how to trigger events using shake detection, in the onShake() method of your JME application, we trigger a new animation of our walking ninja:

```
public void onShake() {
  mAniChannel.setAnim("Spin");
}
```

To avoid that the ninja now spins all the time; we will switch to the walking animation after the spin animation has ended:

```
public void onAnimCycleDone(AnimControl control, AnimChannel
  channel, String animName) {
if(animName.contains("Spin")) {
    mAniChannel.setAnim("Walk");
  }
}
```

If you start your app now and shake the device along the viewing direction, you should see how the ninja stops walking and makes a gentle spin, just as shown in the following figure:

Summary

In this chapter, we've introduced you to three interaction techniques, suitable for a wide variety of AR applications. Picking allows you to select 3D objects by touching the screen, just like you would in 2D selection. Proximity-based camera techniques allow you to experiment with the distance and orientation of your device to trigger application events. Finally, we've showed you a simple example of a 3D gesture detection method to add even more interaction possibilities into your application. These techniques should serve as building blocks for you to create your own interaction methods, targeted to your specific application scenario. In the final chapter, we will introduce some advanced techniques and further reading to help you get the best out of your Augmented Reality applications.

7
Further Reading and Tips

In this final chapter, we will present you with tips and links to more advanced techniques to improve any AR application's development. We will introduce content management techniques such as multi-targets and cloud recognition, as well as advanced interaction techniques.

Managing your content

For computer-vision-based AR, we showed you how to build applications using a single target. However, there might be scenarios in which you need to use several markers at once. Just think of augmenting a room for which you would need at least one target on each wall, or you may want your application to be able to recognize and augment hundreds of different product packages. The former case can be achieved by tracking multiple targets that have a common coordinate frame, and the latter use case can be achieved by using the power of cloud recognition. We will briefly discuss both of them in the following sections.

Multi-targets

Multi-targets are more than a collection of several individual images. They realize a single and consistent coordinate system where a handheld device can be tracked. This allows for continuous augmentation of the scene as long as even a single target is visible. The main challenges of creating multi-targets lie in defining the common coordinate system (which you will do only once) and maintaining the relative poses of those targets during the operation of the device.

To create a common coordinate system, you have to specify the translation and orientation of all image targets with respect to a common origin. Vuforia™ gives you an option to even build commonly used multi-targets such as cubes or cuboids without getting into the details of specifying the entire target transforms. In the Vuforia™ Target Manager, you can simply add a cube (equal length, height, and width) or cuboids (different length, height, and width) to a target that has its coordinate origin at the (invisible) center of the cuboids. All you have to do is to specify one extend to three extends of the cuboids and add individual images for all the sides of your targets, as shown in the following figure:

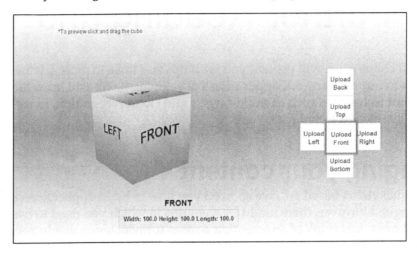

If you want to create more complex multi-targets, for example, for tracking an entire room, you have to take a slightly different approach. You first upload all the images you want to use for the multi-target into a single device database inside the Vuforia™ Target Manager. After, you have downloaded the device database to your development machine, you can then modify the downloaded `<database >.xml` file to add the names of the individual image targets and their translations and orientations relative to the coordinate origin. A sample XML file can be found in the Vuforia™ knowledge base under `https://developer.vuforia.com/resources/dev-guide/creating-multi-target-xml-file`.

Note that you can only have a maximum of 100 targets in your device database, and hence your multi-target can maximally consist of only that number of image targets. Also note that changing the position of image targets during the runtime (for example, opening a product packaging) will inhibit consistent tracking of your coordinate system, that is, the defined spatial relationships between the individual target elements would not be valid anymore. This can even lead to complete failure of tracking. If you want to use individual moving elements as part of your application, you have to define them in addition to the multi-target as separate image targets.

Cloud recognition

As mentioned in the preceding section, you can only use up to 100 images simultaneously in your Vuforia™ application. This limitation can be overcome by using cloud databases. The basic idea here is that you query a cloud service with a camera image, and (if the target is recognized in the cloud), handle the tracking of the recognized target locally on your device. The major benefit of this approach is that you can recognize up to one million images that should be sufficient for most application scenarios. However, this benefit does not come for free. As the recognition happens in the cloud, your client has to be connected to the Internet, and the response time can take up to several seconds (typically around two to three seconds).

Unlike, in the case of recognition, image databases stored on the device typically only take about 60 to 100 milliseconds. To make it easier to upload many images for the cloud recognition, you do not even have to use the Vuforia™ online target manager website but can use a specific web API—the Vuforia™ Web Services API—that can be found under the following URL: `https://developer.vuforia.com/resources/dev-guide/managing-targets-cloud-database-using-developer-api`. You can find further information about using cloud recognition in the Vuforia™ knowledge base by visiting `https://developer.vuforia.com/resources/dev-guide/cloud-targets`.

Improving recognition and tracking

If you want to create your own natural feature-tracking targets, it is important to design them in a way that they can be well recognized and tracked by the AR system. The basics of natural feature targets were explained in the *Understanding natural feature tracking targets* section of *Chapter 5, Same as Hollywood – Virtual on Physical Objects*. The basic requirement for well-traceable targets is that they possess a high number of local features. But how do you go along if your target is not well recognized? To a certain extent, you can improve the tracking by using the forthcoming tips.

First, you want to make sure that your images have enough local contrast. A good indicator for the overall contrast in your target is to have a look at the histogram of its greyscale representation in any photo editing software such as GIMP or Photoshop. You generally want a widely distributed histogram instead of one with few spikes, as shown in the following figure:

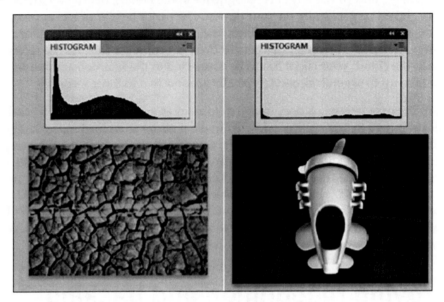

To increase the local contrast in your images, you can use the photo editor of your choice and apply unsharpening mask filters or clarity filters, such as in Adobe Lightroom.

In addition, to avoid resampling artifacts in the Vuforia™ target creation process, make sure to upload your individual images with an exact image width of 320 px. This will avoid aliasing effects and lowering the local feature count due to automatic server-side resizing of your images. By improving the rendering, Vuforia™ will rescale your images to have a maximum extend of 320 px for the longest image side.

During the course of this book, we used different types of 3D models in our sample applications, including basic primitives (such as our colored cube or sphere) or more advanced 3D models (such as the ninja model). For all of them, we didn't really consider the realistic aspect, including the light condition. Any desktop or mobile 3D application will always consider how the rendering looks realistic. This photorealistic quest always passes through the quality of the geometry of the model, the definition of their appearance (material reflectance properties), and how they interact with light (shading and illumination).

Photorealistic rendering will expose properties such as occlusion (what is in front of, behind something), shadows (from the illumination), support for a range of realistic material (developed with shader technology), or more advanced properties such as supporting global illumination.

When you develop your AR applications, you should also consider photorealistic rendering. However, things are a bit more complicated because in AR, you not only consider the virtual aspect (for example, a desktop 3D game) but also the real aspect. Supporting photorealism in AR will imply that you consider **how real (R) environments and virtual (V) environments** also interact during the rendering that can be simplified as follows through four different cases:

1. V→V
2. V→R
3. R→V
4. R→R

The easiest thing you can do is support V→V, which means that you enable any of the advanced rendering techniques in your 3D rendering engine. For computer-vision-based applications, it will mean that everything looks realistic on your target. For sensor-based applications, it will mean that your virtual object seems realistic between each other.

A second easy step, especially for computer-vision-based applications, is to support V→R using a plane technique. If you have a target, you can create a semi-transparent version of it and add it to your virtual scene. If you have shadows enabled, it will seem that the shadow is projecting on to your target, creating a simple illusion of V→R. You can refer to the following paper which will provide you with some technical solutions to this problem:

- Refer to *A real-time shadow approach for an augmented reality application using shadow volumes. VRST 2003: 56-65* by *Michael Haller, Stephan Drab,* and *Werner Hartmann.*

Handling R→V is a bit more complicated and still a difficult research topic. For example, support illumination of virtual objects by physical light sources requires a lot of effort.

Instead, occlusion is easy to implement for R→V. Occlusion in the case of R→V can happen if, for example, a physical object (such as a **can**) is placed in front of your virtual object. In standard AR, you always render the virtual content in front of the video, so your **can** will appear to be behind even though it can be in front of your target.

A simple technique to reproduce this effect is sometimes referred to as **phantom object**. You need to create a virtual counterpart of your physical object, such as a cylinder, to represent your can. Place this virtual counterpart at the same position as the physical one and do a **depth-only rendering**. Depth-only rendering is available in a large range of libraries, and it's related to the color mask where, when you render anything, you can decide which channel to render. Commonly, you have the combination of red, green, blue, and depth. So, you need to deactivate the first three channels and only activate depth. It will render some sort of phantom object (no color but only depth), and via the standard rendering pipeline, the video will not be occluded anymore where you have your real object, and occlusion will look realistic; see, for example, `http://hal.inria.fr/docs/00/53/75/15/PDF/occlusionCollaborative.pdf`.

This is the simple case; when you have a dynamic object, things are way more complicated, and you need to be able to track your objects, to update their phantom models, and to be able to get a photorealistic rendering.

Advanced interaction techniques

In the preceding chapter, we looked at some simple interaction techniques, that included ray picking (via touch interaction), sensor interaction, or camera to target proximity. There are a large number of other interaction techniques that can be used in Augmented Reality.

One standard technique that we will also find on other mobile user interfaces, is a **virtual control pad**. As a mobile phone limits access to additional control devices, such as a joypad or joystick, you can emulate their behavior via a touch interface. With this technique, you can display a virtual controller on your screen and analyze the touch in this area as being equivalent to controlling a control pad. It's easy to implement and enhance the basic ray-casting technique. Control pads are generally displayed near the border of the screen, adapting to the form factor and grasping the gesture you make when you hold the device, so you can hold the device with your hand and naturally move your finger on the screen.

Another technique that is really popular in Augmented Reality is **Tangible User Interface (TUI)**. When we created the sample using the concept of a camera to target proximity, we practically implemented a Tangible User Interface. The idea of a TUI is to use a physical object for supporting interaction. The concept was largely developed and enriched by *Iroshi Ishii* from the Tangible Media Group at MIT — the website to refer to is `http://tangible.media.mit.edu/`. *Mark Billinghurst* during his Ph.D. applied this concept to Augmented Reality and demonstrated a range of dedicated interaction techniques with it.

The first type of TUI AR is **local interaction**, where you can, for example, use two targets for interaction. Similar to the way we detected the distance between the camera and target in our `ProximityBasedJME` project, you can replicate the same idea with two targets. You can detect whether two targets are close to each other, aligned in the same direction, and trigger some actions with it. You can use this type of interaction for card-based games when you want cards to interact with each other, or games that include puzzles where users need to combine different cards together, and so on.

A second type of TUI AR is **global interaction** where you will also use two or more targets, but one of the targets will become *special*. What you do in this case is define a target as being a base target, and all the other targets refer to it. To implement it, you just compute the local transformation of the other targets to the base target, with the base target behind and defined as your origin. With this, it's really easy to place targets on the main target, somehow defining some kind of ground plane and performing a range of different types of interaction with it. *Mark Billinghurst* introduced a famous derivate version of it, for performing paddle-based interaction. In this case, one of the targets is used as a paddle and can be used to interact on the ground plane—you can touch the ground plane, have the paddle at a specific position on the ground plane, or even detect a simple gesture with it (shake the paddle, tilt the paddle, and so on). To set up mobile AR, you need to consider the fact that end users hold a device and can't perform complex gestures, but with a mobile phone, interaction with one hand is still possible. Refer to the following technical papers:

- *Tangible augmented reality. ACM SIGGRAPH ASIA (2008): 1-10* by *Mark Billinghurst, Hirokazu Kato,* and *Ivan Poupyrev.*

- *Designing augmented reality interfaces. ACM Siggraph Computer Graphics 39.1 (2005): 17-22* by *Mark Billinghurst, Raphael Grasset,* and *Julian Looser.*

Global interaction with a TUI, in a sense, can be defined as interaction *behind the screen*, while virtual control pad can be seen as interaction *in front of the screen*. This is another way to classify interaction with a mobile, which brings us to the third category of interaction techniques: **touch interaction on the target**. The Vuforia™ library implements, for example, the concept of virtual buttons. A specific area on your target can be used to place the controller (for example, buttons, sliders, and dial), and users can place their finger on this area and control these elements. The concept behind this uses a time-based approach; if you keep your finger placed on this area for a long time, it simulates a click that you can have on a computer, or a tap you can do on a touch screen. Refer to `https://developer.vuforia.com/resources/sample-apps/virtual-button-sample-app`, for example.

There are other techniques that are investigated in research laboratories, and they will soon become available to the future generation of mobile AR, so you should already think about them also when will be available. One trend is towards 3D gesture interaction or also called **mid-air interaction**. Rather than touching your screen or touching your target, you can imagine making gestures between the device and the target. Having a mobile AR for 3D modeling would be an appropriate technique. 3D gestures have a lot of challenges such as recognizing the hand, the fingers, the gesture, physical engagement that can result in fatigue, and so on. In the near future, this type of interaction, which is already popular on smart home devices (such as Microsoft Kinect), will be available on devices (equipped with 3D sensors).

Summary

In this chapter, we showed you how to go beyond the standard AR applications by using multi-targets or cloud recognition for computer-vision-based AR. We also showed you how you can improve the tracking performance for your image targets. In addition, we introduced you to some advanced rendering techniques for your AR applications. Finally, we also showed you some novel interaction techniques that you can use to create great AR experiences. This chapter concludes your introduction to the world of Augmented Reality development for Android. We hope you are ready to progress onto new levels of AR application development.

Index

Thank you for buying
Augmented Reality for
Android Application Development

About Packt Publishing

Packt, pronounced 'packed', published its first book "*Mastering phpMyAdmin for Effective MySQL Management*" in April 2004 and subsequently continued to specialize in publishing highly focused books on specific technologies and solutions.

Our books and publications share the experiences of your fellow IT professionals in adapting and customizing today's systems, applications, and frameworks. Our solution based books give you the knowledge and power to customize the software and technologies you're using to get the job done. Packt books are more specific and less general than the IT books you have seen in the past. Our unique business model allows us to bring you more focused information, giving you more of what you need to know, and less of what you don't.

Packt is a modern, yet unique publishing company, which focuses on producing quality, cutting-edge books for communities of developers, administrators, and newbies alike. For more information, please visit our website: www.packtpub.com.

About Packt Open Source

In 2010, Packt launched two new brands, Packt Open Source and Packt Enterprise, in order to continue its focus on specialization. This book is part of the Packt Open Source brand, home to books published on software built around Open Source licences, and offering information to anybody from advanced developers to budding web designers. The Open Source brand also runs Packt's Open Source Royalty Scheme, by which Packt gives a royalty to each Open Source project about whose software a book is sold.

Writing for Packt

We welcome all inquiries from people who are interested in authoring. Book proposals should be sent to author@packtpub.com. If your book idea is still at an early stage and you would like to discuss it first before writing a formal book proposal, contact us; one of our commissioning editors will get in touch with you.

We're not just looking for published authors; if you have strong technical skills but no writing experience, our experienced editors can help you develop a writing career, or simply get some additional reward for your expertise.

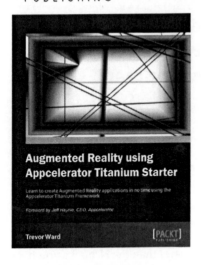

Augmented Reality using Appcelerator Titanium Starter [Instant]

ISBN: 978-1-84969-390-5   Paperback: 52 pages

Learn to create Augmented Reality applications in no time using the Appcelerator Titanium Framework

1. Learn something new in an Instant! A short, fast, focused guide delivering immediate results.

2. Create an open source Augmented Reality Titanium application

3. Build an effective display of multiple points of interest

Augmented Reality with Kinect

ISBN: 978-1-84969-438-4   Paperback: 122 pages

Develop tour own handsfree and attractive augmented reality applications with Microsoft Kinect

1. Understand all major Kinect API features including image streaming, skeleton tracking and face tracking

2. Understand the Kinect APIs with the help of small examples

3. Develop a comparatively complete Fruit Ninja game using Kinect and augmented Reality techniques

Please check **www.PacktPub.com** for information on our titles

Android Development Tools for Eclipse

ISBN: 978-1-78216-110-3   Paperback: 144 pages

Set up, build, and publish Android projects quickly using Android Development Tools for Eclipse

1. Build Android applications using ADT for Eclipse

2. Generate Android application skeleton code using wizards

3. Advertise and monetize your applications

Android Application Programming with OpenCV

ISBN: 978-1-84969-520-6   Paperback: 130 pages

Build Android apps to capture, manipulate, and track objects in 2D and 3D

1. Set up OpenCV and an Android development environment on Windows, Mac, or Linux

2. Capture and display real-time videos and still images

3. Manipulate image data using OpenCV and Apache Commons Math

Please check **www.PacktPub.com** for information on our titles